Sue Stratford

As well as being lucky enough to spend her time thinking up and knitting new designs, Sue also owns and runs *The Knitting Hut*, a small but perfectly formed yarn store in Buckinghamshire. She teaches knitting and crochet workshops as well as offering advice to customers and loves sharing her skills with others. Her mind is always full of new ideas, often inspired by the beautiful yarns stocked in the shop. Sue lives in Milton Keynes with her husband, five children and a selection of pets.

Also by Sue Stratford

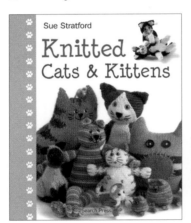

KNITTED
Dogs &
Puppies

KNITTED
Dogs &
Puppies

Sue Stratford

Search Press

First published in 2014

Search Press Limited
Wellwood, North Farm Road,
Tunbridge Wells, Kent TN2 3DR

Text copyright © Sue Stratford 2014

Photographs by Roddy Paine Photographic Studios

Photographs and design copyright © Search Press Ltd 2014

ISBN 978 1 84448 960 2

Suppliers
If you have difficulty in obtaining any of the materials and
equipment mentioned in this book, then please visit the
Search Press website for details of suppliers:
www.searchpress.com

Materials can also be obtained from the author's
own website: www.suestratford.co.uk.

Printed in China

Acknowledgements

Without the help and support of Team Hut this
book would not have been possible; especially
Susan Edwards and Babs Davis, who diligently
test-knitted the dogs and pups.
Thank you also to my ever-patient family who put
up with knitted pups all over the house and to
our dogs, Hector and Hetty, for not thinking they
were for them.
Thanks also to Gavin and Roddy for bringing the
dogs to life in the fantastic photographs. I would
also like to thank Jacky Edwards for her skill and
attention to detail.
Special thanks to Poppy who always gives me her
honest opinion.

Did someone
mention walkies?

Contents

Dress-up Dogs, page 14

Chic Chihuahua, page 40

Outdoors Dog, page 66

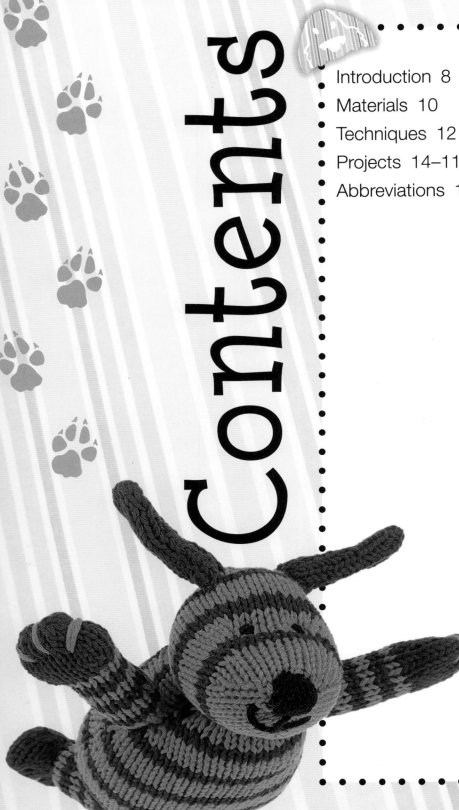

Sweetheart, page 92

Stripy Sausage, page 24

Fluffy Floppy Dog, page 28

Circus Dogs, page 32

Black and White Terriers, page 36

Mischief-makers, page 46

Bullseye, page 50

Stripes, page 56

Pink Poodle, page 60

Christmas Dog, page 72

Danger Dog, page 78

Best in Show, page 84

Teeny Tiny Doglet, page 88

Labrador, page 96

Bonnie Prince Charlie, page 100

Cuddle Pup, page 106

Doggy Treats, page 110

Introduction

I have had great fun thinking up and knitting these cute and cuddly pups. Each one has his or her own character and I love that they make people smile when they see them. They are a collection of dog 'characters' instead of breeds but there are a few favourites included such as a chihuahua on page 40 and a King Charles Spaniel on page 100. The yarns I have chosen for each makes them come alive and the designs can be easily adapted to make your own personalised pooch.

Before you start knitting it is worth reading through the abbreviations and techniques as some of these are key to getting your dog to look extra special. The way I have worked the increases (working a backwards loop) is explained on the abbreviations page and is a great way of increasing which produces a virtually invisible finished result.

I also use a technique with which you may be familiar, the three needle cast off (US three needle bind off).This is a really neat way of closing a seam at the end of your knitted piece and it also means one less seam to sew up!

Get off, it's mine!

8

Get your
knitting needles
ready — here
we come!

I have also suggested leaving a length of yarn on some pieces to enable you to sew the piece in place and, in the case of the nose, to help embroider the mouth. This will save fastening off the end of your yarn and then joining a new one.

Another helpful idea is to sew each piece of the dog together as you finish them. This helps if you have lots of pieces and saves you getting to the end and not knowing which piece is which.

The sewing up is what gives your dog his character and so it is worth spending some time getting the features right. I suggest using pins to check the placement of the eyes before sewing them in place.

There are quite a few projects in the book that are suitable for relatively new knitters such as the Terriers on page 36 and Cuddle Pup on page 106, so there is something for everyone.

Every dog needs a bone, so I have included a selection of treats like bones, bowls and even a string of sausages for your playful pup.

I have loved making all the dogs in this book; their expressions make me smile and they are all so different. For pure cuddliness I think that Fluffy Floppy Dog on page 28 has to be one of my favourites, and Danger Dog, on page 78, never fails to put a smile on my face. Whichever you choose, I hope you enjoy making your own special dog.

Materials

The knitting materials you will need to knit the dogs in this book are listed here, along with a few notes to help explain how to use some of the yarns, needles and other equipment.

Yarns

The yarns used have been chosen with the character of each dog in mind. However, you can easily use different yarns to give your dog a completely original look. Simply look at the ply or the type of yarn used (sportweight, Aran, laceweight and so on) and this will give you an idea of what thickness to go for. Alternatively, choose a different weight of yarn that is close to the original, but make sure you adjust the needle size used accordingly. This will prevent the shape from distorting when you stuff the dog with toy filling, and the toy filling will not show through the stitches.

The materials list for each project gives the types, colours and amounts of the yarns used in metres and yards; unless only a small amount is used for details, such as for the noses. The majority of the projects require a small amount of black 4-ply (fingering) yarn for such details. One ball will provide enough yarn for a number of projects.

Knitting needles

You can use any type of knitting needle to make these cuddly characters. For the smaller projects I prefer to use double-pointed needles as they are shorter than standard needles and work well when you have relatively few stitches. Where a pattern requires stitch markers, this is stated at the beginning of the pattern.

Stitch holders

Stitch holders are used in a few of the patterns to 'rest' stitches on while you continue with a different part of the dog. If you have not used them before do not worry; just slide the stitches on to the holder without twisting them and leave them there until the pattern asks you to use them again, then slide them back on to your knitting needle. If you do not have stitch holders, you can use a length of yarn instead.

Filling

If the dog is intended as a toy, ensure that the stuffing you use is child safe. Before you stuff your dog, tease the filling out to stop lumps forming and give an even result. Some of the dogs have weighting beads in their bodies or arms and legs. For safety, sew a little cloth bag to put the beads in to stop them escaping, then put the bag of beads into the arm, leg or body before stuffing. Where weighting beads are used, they are listed at the start of the project.

Sewing needles

You will need a darning needle to sew the dogs together. The size of needle used depends on the weight of the yarn – the thicker the yarn, the larger the needle you will need. Remember to pull the sewing yarn from the base near the knitting when stitching to stop the yarn stretching and breaking. Some patterns require a sewing needle for embroidery or for sewing on small eyes. Where needed, they are listed at the start of the project.

Scissors

These are always an essential in any knitter's kit. Try to find a small pair to keep in your knitting bag for snipping the yarn when knitting separate arms, legs and bodies. Make sure they are nice and sharp.

Buttons and beads

Some of the dogs have beads as eyes. Make sure they are sewn on securely and use the appropriate size for your dog. If the dog is intended as a toy, you can embroider eyes using black yarn. French knots (see page 12) are a great alternative to beads.

Techniques

I-cord

To make an i-cord, cast on your stitches using double-pointed needles, knit them and slide them to the other end of the same needle. Pull the yarn around the back of the needle and knit the stitches again. Repeat these instructions until the cord is long enough. By pulling the yarn behind the stitches on the needle, you close the 'gap' and give the appearance of French knitting. Alternatively, you can work the stitches in stocking stitch and sew up the seam.

Mattress stitch

This is a really neat way to join two pieces of stocking stitch together. The seam is practically invisible and not at all bulky. Begin by laying the work side by side with the right side facing you. Slip your needle through the horizontal bar between the first and second stitch of the first row on one piece and then repeat this process on the opposite piece. Work back and forth up this line of stitches for about 2.5cm (1in). Gently pull the yarn in the direction of the seam (upwards) and you will see the two sets of stitches join together. Repeat this process until you reach the top of the seam.

Wrap and turn

This technique ensures you do not end up with a 'hole' in your knitting when working short row shaping and turning your work mid-row. Slip the next stitch on your left needle to the right needle. Move the yarn to the other side of the work, between the needles. Slip stitch back to the left-hand needle. Turn work. The stitch now has a 'wrap' of yarn around it.

Fair Isle technique

Fair Isle is a method of knitting with two colours, in which only a few stitches in the contrasting colour are used. The yarn not being knitted is carried loosely across the back of the work. It is best to carry the contrasting yarn over five or six stitches and then loop the main colour around it. This will secure it to the back of the work and avoid large loops appearing. If you carry the yarn loosely, the work will be neater on the RS.

French knots

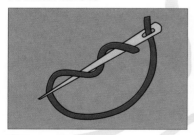 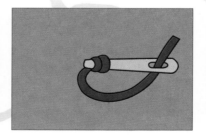 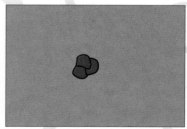

1. Bring the sewing needle through to the front of the work and wind the yarn around the needle twice.

2. Take the needle through the work, half a stitch away, holding the loops around the needle with your fingers while pulling the yarn through to the back of your work.

3. Pull the thread into a knot and fasten off.

Three needle cast off

A few of the dogs' heads are knitted from the nose towards the back of the head. The cast-off edge then forms the back of the head. By using this technique to cast off, not only do you achieve a really neat finish, but there is one less seam to sew up! You can also use this technique on some of the dogs' legs. This is noted on the patterns.

1. Divide the remaining stitches evenly between two needles. Fold the knitting so that the right sides are together.

2. Using a third needle, knit the first stitch from each needle together.

3. Knit the next stitch from each needle together. Cast off the first stitch in the usual way, by lifting it over the second stitch.

4. Repeat until all the stitches have been cast off. Turn the piece the right way out before sewing up.

Shaping the nose

When I was making the dogs I found that sometimes the nose could end up too 'pointy'. By gathering the tip of the nose as shown below, you get a much better shape. Once the knitted nose is sewn on top, all the gathering is invisible.

1. Once you have sewn up the head seam to the point shown, run a length of yarn around the hole this leaves, two or three rows back from the edge (I have used red yarn here for clarity).

2. Tuck the two or three rows inside and gently pull the yarn to gather the wool into shape.

3. Secure the yarn and trim away the excess.

13

Dress-up Dogs

This cute pair of pups is knitted using a fluffy bouclé yarn to make them very tactile. The pirate jumper is knitted using the Fair Isle technique (see page 12) and his mermaid friend's tail can be taken off.

Materials
60m (66yd) of 10-ply (Aran) alpaca bouclé yarn
Small amount of black 4-ply (fingering) yarn
Toy filling
Two 6mm (¼in) black beads
Black sewing cotton and sewing needle

Needles
4.5mm (UK 7, US 7) knitting needles
2.75mm (UK 12, US 2) knitting needles

Tension
Approximately 18–20 sts measured over 10cm (4in) and worked in SS using 4.5mm knitting needles (UK 7, US 7) and 10-ply (Aran) alpaca bouclé yarn

Size
18cm (7in) from the top of the head to the bottom of the feet

Notes
These dogs are knitted in SS. When you sew each one together, place the WS on the outside as this is the fluffier side.

The materials listed above are sufficient for one of the dogs. The materials for the costumes are listed with the patterns later.

Body
Using 10-ply (Aran) yarn and 4.5mm (UK 7, US 7) knitting needles cast on 14 sts.
Next row: K3, Kfb, K6, Kfb, K3 [16 sts].
Next row: P4, Pfb, P6, Pfb, P4 [18 sts].
Next row: K4, Kfb, K8, Kfb, K4 [20 sts].
Next row: P5, Pfb, P8, Pfb, P5 [22 sts].
Next row: K5, Kfb, K10, Kfb, K5 [24 sts].
Next row: P6, Pfb, P10, Pfb, P6 [26 sts].
Next row: K6, Kfb, K12, Kfb, K6 [28 sts].
Next row: P7, Pfb, P12, Pfb, P7 [30 sts].
Work 12 rows in SS.
Next row: K6, K2tog, K14, K2tog, K6 [28 sts].
Purl 1 row.
Next row: K6, K2tog, K12, K2tog, K6 [26 sts].
Purl 1 row.
Next row: K4, (K2tog) twice, K10, (K2tog) twice, K4 [22 sts].
Next row: P3, (P2tog) twice, P8, (P2tog) twice, P3 [18 sts].
Next row: K2, (K2tog) twice, K6, (K2tog) twice, K2 [14 sts].
Purl 1 row.
Cast off.

Head
Using 10-ply (Aran) yarn and 4.5mm (UK 7, US 7) knitting needles, cast on 14 sts and, starting with a knit row, work 6 rows in SS, ending with a purl row.
Next row: K5, (Kfb) four times, K5 [18 sts].
Purl 1 row.
Next row: K5, (Kfb) eight times, K5 [26 sts].
Work 3 rows in SS.
Next row: K5, (K2tog) eight times, K5 [18 sts].
Purl 1 row.
Next row: K5, (K2tog) four times, K5 [14 sts].
Purl 1 row.
Cast off using the three needle cast off technique (see page 13).

Legs (make two)

Using 10-ply (Aran) yarn and 4.5mm (UK 7, US 7) knitting needles, cast on 8 sts.

Starting with a knit row, work 4cm (1½in) in SS, ending with a purl row.

Next row: K3, M1, K2, M1, K3 [10 sts].

Next row: P4, M1, P2, M1, P4 [12 sts].

Next row: K5, M1, K2, M1, K5 [14 sts].

Next row: P6, M1, P2, M1, P6 [16 sts].

Next row: K7, M1, K2, M1, K7 [18 sts].

Work 3 rows in SS.

Cast off using the three needle cast off technique (see page 13).

Arms (make two)

Using 10-ply (Aran) yarn and 4.5mm (UK 7, US 7) knitting needles, cast on 7 sts and, starting with a knit row, work 3cm (1⅛in) in SS, ending with a purl row.

Next row: (K1, M1) six times, K1 [13 sts].

Work 5 rows in SS.

Next row: (K2tog) three times, K1, (K2tog) three times [7 sts].

Purl 1 row.

Leave a length of yarn for sewing up.

Floppy ears (make two)

Worked in GS.

Using 10-ply (Aran) yarn and 4.5mm (UK 7, US 7) knitting needles, cast on 5 sts and work 3cm (1⅛in) in GS.

Next row: K1, M1, K to last st, M1, K1 [7 sts].

Knit 2 rows.

Next row: K1, K2tog, K1, K2tog, K1 [5 sts].

Knit 1 row.

Cast off.

Nose

Using black 4-ply (fingering) yarn and 2.75mm (UK 12, US 2) knitting needles, cast on 3 sts and purl 1 row.

Next row: K1, M1, K1, M1, K1 [5 sts].

Work 2 rows in SS.

Next row: P2tog, P1, P2togtbl [3 sts].

Next row: Sl1, K2tog, psso [1 st].

Cast off, leaving a length of yarn sufficient to embroider the mouth.

Tail

Using 10-ply (Aran) yarn and 4.5mm (UK 7, US 7) knitting needles, cast on 6 sts and work 3cm (1⅛in) in SS.

Thread yarn through sts and leave a length of yarn for sewing up.

Making up

To make up the body, with the WS on the outside and the cast-off edge at the bottom, sew the back body seam, stuffing with toy filling as you go. This seam will be at the back. Sew the bottom seam closed from side to side.

To make up the head, place the cast-off edge at the back of the head. Sew up the seam (with the WS on the outside) which will go underneath the head, stuffing with toy filling as you go. Sew the cast-on edges together up to the nose. To finish the head, follow the instructions on page 13 to gather the nose.

Pin the 6mm (¼in) black beads in place as eyes, using the picture for guidance, then sew them in place. Run a thread from the back of the eye down to the base of the head and pull slightly, secure. Repeat for the second eye. This gives the eyes a much more realistic look.

Sew the nose in place and embroider the mouth using the length of yarn left at the end of the nose. Sew the ears in place, using the pictures for guidance. Pin the completed head to the body and sew it in place.

Fold one leg in half with the WS on the outside. Sew the leg seam, stuffing gently with toy filling as you go. The long seam will be at the back of the leg. Sew the seam at the top of the leg together from side to side. Repeat for the second leg.

Using the length of yarn remaining from gathering the cast-off edge, sew along the seam of one arm, stuffing gently with toy filling as you go. Repeat for the second arm.

Pin the arms in place on to the side of the body with the seam underneath the arm. Sew in place. Pin the legs in place on to the body, using the pictures for guidance, then sew them in place.

Using the length of yarn remaining from gathering the cast-off edge of the tail, sew along the seam and sew it to the back of the body.

Mermaid costume

Materials
110m (120½yd) green 5-ply (sportweight) yarn
Small amount pale pink 5-ply (sportweight) yarn
Small amount of toy filling
Four 6mm (¼in) pearl beads
Cream sewing cotton and sewing needle

Needles
3.25mm (UK 10, US 3) knitting needles

Tension
25 sts measured over 10cm (4in) and worked in SS using 3.25mm (UK 10, US 3) knitting needles and 5-ply (sportweight) yarn

Main tail
Using green 5-ply (sportweight) yarn and 3.25mm (UK 10, US 3) knitting needles, cast on 36 sts and, starting with a knit row, work 4 rows in SS.
Next row: (K2tog, yo) seventeen times, K2 [36 sts]. This row forms picot edge.
Work 21 rows in SS.
Next row: K8, K2tog, K16, K2tog, K8 [34 sts].
Work 3 rows in SS.
Next row: K7, K2tog, K16, K2tog, K7 [32 sts].
Work 3 rows in SS.
Next row: K7, K2tog, K14, K2tog, K7 [30 sts].
Work 3 rows in SS.

Next row: K7, K2tog, K12, K2tog, K7 [28 sts].
Work 3 rows in SS.
Next row: K5, (K2tog) twice, K10, (K2tog) twice, K5 [24 sts].
Work 3 rows in SS.
Next row: K4, (K2tog) twice, K8, (K2tog) twice, K4. [20 sts].
Work 3 rows in SS.
Next row: K3, (K2tog) twice, K6, (K2tog) twice, K3 [16 sts].
Work 3 rows in SS.
Next row: K2, (K2tog) twice, K4, (K2tog) twice, K2 [12 sts].
Purl 1 row.
Next row: K1, (K2tog) twice, K2, (K2tog) twice, K1 [8 sts].
Purl 1 row.
Cast off.

Scales
Using green 5-ply (sportweight) yarn and 3.25mm (UK 10, US 3) knitting needles, cast on 5 sts and purl 1 row.
* **Row 1:** K1, M1, K to the end of the row [6 sts].
Row 2: P to last st, M1, P1 [7 sts].
Row 3: K1, M1, K to the end of the row [8 sts].
Row 4: P to last st, M1, P1 [9 sts].
Row 5: K1, M1, K to the end of the row. [10 sts].
Row 6: Purl 1 row.
Row 7: K1, ssK, K to end of row [9 sts].
Row 8: P to last 3 sts, ssP, P1 [8 sts].
Row 9: K1, ssK, K to end of row [7 sts].
Row 10: P to last 3 sts, ssP, P1 [6 sts].
Row 11: K1, ssK, K to end of row [5 sts].
Purl 1 row. *
This forms one scale. When you have knitted the right amount of scales cast off. Using the instructions between * and *, make the following rows of scales:
First row (top row): 5 scales.
Second row: 5 scales.
Third row: 5 scales.
Fourth row: 4 scales.
Fifth row: 3 scales.
Sixth row: 2 scales.

Fin (make four)

Using green 5-ply (sportweight) yarn and 3.25mm (UK 10, US 3) knitting needles, cast on 5 sts.

Row 1: (P1, K1tbl) twice, P1.

Row 2: (K1, P1tbl) twice, K1.

Row 3: P1, M1, K1tbl, P1, K1tbl, M1, P1 [7 sts].

Row 4: K2, P1tbl, K1, P1tbl, K2.

Row 5: P2, M1, K1tbl, P1, K1tbl, M1, P2 [9 sts].

Row 6: (K1, P1tbl) four times, K1.

Row 7: (P1, K1tbl) four times, P1.

Row 8: K1, M1, (P1tbl, K1) three times, P1tbl, M1, K1 [11 sts].

Row 9: P2, (K1tbl, P1) three times, K1tbl, P2.

Row 10: K1, M1, (K1, P1tbl) four times, K1, M1, K1 [13 sts].

Row 11: (P1, K1tbl) six times, P1.

Row 12: (K1tbl, P1) six times, K1tbl.

Rep rows 11 and 12 once more.

Rep row 11 once more.

Row 16: P2tog, (K1tbl, P1) four times, K1tbl, P2tog [11 sts].

Row 17: K3, P1tbl, K3, P1tbl, K3.

Row 18: P1, P2tog, K1tbl, P1, p2tog, K1tbl, P2tog, P1 [8 sts].

Row 19: (K2tog, P1tbl) twice, K2tog [5 sts].

Row 20: (P1, K1tbl) twice, P1.

Cast off.

Making up

Starting with the main part of the tail and with WS on the outside, fold the top four rows over and sew in place, so that the eyelet row forms a picot edging along the top edge of the tail.

Sew the back seam of the tail. The seam will be at the back of the tail.

With WS together sew two fin pieces together stuffing gently with toy filling. Repeat for the second fin.

Sew a stuffed fin to each side of the bottom edge of the tail, using the picture for guidance, and sewing the cast-off edge to the tail.

Lightly press the scale rows. Starting with the bottom row, pin in place (see order of scales on previous page) so that each row overlaps. The top row should rest on the top seam. Sew each row in place, easing to fit. The cast-on and cast-off edges should be at the back.

Bikini shells (make two)

Using pale pink 5-ply (sportweight) yarn and 3.25mm (UK 10, US 3) knitting needles, cast on 6 sts and knit 2 rows.

Cast off. This forms the bottom of one shell.

With RS facing, pick up and K 3 sts in the middle of the row, leaving a stitch and a half each side.

Next row: P1, M1, P1, M1, P1 [5 sts].

Next row: K1, M1, K3, M1, K1 [7 sts].

Work 3 rows in SS.

Next row: ssK, K3, K2tog [5 sts].

Next row: P2tog, P1, P2togtbl [3 sts].

Cast off.

Halter neck strap

Using green 5-ply (sportweight) yarn and 3.25mm (UK 10, US 3) knitting needles, cast on 20 sts and work 2 rows in SS.

Cast off.

Lower strap

Using green 5-ply (sportweight) yarn and 3.25mm (UK 10, US 3) knitting needles, cast on 50 sts and work 2 rows in SS.

Cast off.

Making up

Lightly press the shell pieces and sew three straight stitches along the top of the GS section of each shell, using the picture as guidance.

Pin each shell in place on the lower strap, with the two ends at the back and the shells evenly spaced at the front. Use the picture for guidance. Sew the lower edge of the shells to the top edge of the strap.

Sew a small loop on one end of the strap then use cream sewing cotton to sew a pearl bead to the other end.

Sew each end of the halter neck strap to the top back edge of each shell.

Using cream sewing cotton, sew a group of three pearls to the centre front of the bikini strap as shown in the picture.

Pirate costume

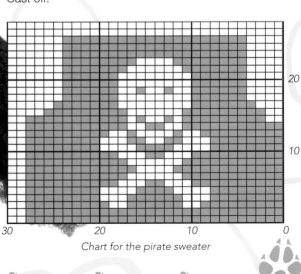

Materials

45m (49¼yd) of black 4-ply (fingering) yarn
10m (11yd) of red 4-ply (fingering) yarn
Small amount of cream 4-ply (fingering) yarn
Small amount of red 4-ply (fingering) yarn
Small length of black elastic

Needles

3.25mm (UK 10, US 3) knitting needles

Tension

28 sts measured over 10cm (4in) and worked in SS using 3.25mm (UK 10, US 3) knitting needles and black 4-ply (fingering yarn)

Eye patch

Using black 4-ply (fingering) yarn and 3.25mm (UK 10, US 3) knitting needles, cast on 3 sts and K 2 rows.
Next row: (K1, M1) twice, K1 [5 sts].
Knit 2 rows.
Cast off.
Measure a piece of elastic to go around the dog's head. Sew each end of the black elastic at the back of the eye patch.

Sweater (front)

Using black 4-ply (fingering) yarn and 3.25mm (UK 10, US 3) knitting needles, cast on 28 sts and work four rows in K2, P2 rib.
Following the chart for the pirate skull and crossbones and using the Fair Isle technique (see page 12), work as follows:
Starting with a knit row, work 14 rows in SS.
Cast off 2 sts at the beginning of the next two rows [24 sts].
Next row: K2, ssK, K to last 4 sts, K2tog, K2 [22 sts].
Next row: P2, P2tog, P to last 4 sts, P2togtbl, P2 [20 sts].
Work 8 rows in SS. *
Next row: K7, turn, leaving rem 13 sts on the needle.
Next row: P1, P2tog, P4 [6 sts].
Next row: K3, K2tog, K1 [5 sts].
Cast off.
With RS facing, rejoin yarn to rem 13 sts and cast off 6 sts, K to end of row [7 sts].
Next row: P4, P2togtbl, P1 [6 sts].
Next row: K1, ssK, K3 [5 sts].
Cast off.

Chart for the pirate sweater

Sweater (back)

Work as for front to * and continue as follows.

Next row: K8, turn, leaving rem 12 sts on the needle.

Next row: P1, P2tog, P5 [7 sts].

Next row: K4, K2tog, K1 [6 sts].

Next row: P1, P2tog, P3 [5 sts].

Cast off.

With RS facing rejoin yarn to rem 12 sts and cast off 4 sts, K to end of row [8 sts].

Next row: P5, P2togtbl, P1 [7 sts].

Next row: K1, ssK, K4 [6 sts].

Next row: P3, P2tog, P1 [5 sts].

Cast off.

Join the right shoulder seam and pick up and K 12 sts around the front neck shaping. Pick up and K 12 sts around the back of the neck shaping [24 sts].

Work four rows in K2, P2 rib.

Cast off loosely and evenly.

Sew left shoulder and neckband seam.

Sleeves

Taking the joined front and back of the jumper, pick up and K 24 sts along the edge of one armhole.

Starting with a purl row, work 3 rows in SS.

Next row: K1, ssK, K to last 3 sts, K2tog, K1 [22 sts].

Work 3 rows in SS.

Rep the last four rows once more [20 sts].

Work 4 rows in K2, P2 rib.

Cast off.

Repeat for the second sleeve.

Sew each underarm and side seam.

Bandana

Using red 4-ply (fingering) yarn and 3.25mm (UK 10, US 3) knitting needles, cast on 3 sts.

Next row: (K1, M1) twice, K1 [5 sts].

Next row: K2, P1, K2.

Next row: K1, M1, K to last st, M1, K1 [7 sts].

Next row: K2, P3, K2.

Next row: K2, M1, K to last 2 sts, M1, K2 [9 sts].

Next row: K2, P5, K2.

Next row: K2, M1, K to last 2 sts, M1, K2 [11 sts].

Next row: K2, P7, K2.

Next row: K2, M1, K to last 2 sts, M1, K2 [13 sts].

Next row: K2, P9, K2.

Next row: K2, M1, K to last 2 sts, M1, K2 [15 sts].

Next row: K2, P11, K2.

Working in GS from now on, cast on 12 sts at the beginning of the next two rows [39 sts].

Knit 2 rows. Cast off.

Using cream 4-ply (fingering) yarn, embroider spots on to the bandana using French knots (see page 12).

Flag

Using red 4-ply (fingering) yarn and 2.75mm (UK 12, US 2) knitting needles, cast on 14 sts and work 4 rows in GS.

Next row: Knit all sts.

Next row: K3, P to last 3 sts, K3.

Rep last two rows once more.

Next row: K2, ssK, K to last 4 sts, K2tog, K2 [12 sts].

Next row: K3, P to last 3 sts, K3.

Rep last two rows three more times [6 sts].

Next row: K1, (K2tog) twice, K1 [4 sts].

Next row: K2tog twice [2 sts].

Thread yarn through rem 2 sts and fasten.

Using cream 4-ply (fingering) yarn, embroider spots on to the flag using French knots (see page 12).

If you want to attach your flag to a stick as on page 15 (I used a dog treat), then use loops of red yarn to secure it.

Stripy Sausage

Stripy Sausage is a useful little chap: lay him in front of a door to keep your draughts out! He is a fat little sausage dog whose legs are sticking out in front and behind him, just like my dog when he is fast asleep. You can vary the colours used to fit in with your own colour scheme.

Materials
- 375m (410yd) brown 5-ply (sportweight) yarn (used double throughout)
- The following amounts of 5-ply (sportweight) yarn (used double throughout): 50m (55yd) purple, 34m (37¼yd) turquoise, 39m (43yd) teal, 24m (26¼yd) light brown, 44m (48¼yd) bright green and 60m (66yd) red
- Small amount of black 4-ply (fingering) yarn
- Stitch holders
- Toy filling
- Two 10mm (⅜in) black shanked buttons

Needles
- 4.5mm (UK 7, US 7) knitting needles
- 2.75mm (UK 12, US 2) knitting needles

Tension
18 sts measured over 10cm (4in) using 4.5mm (UK 7, US 7) knitting needles and 5-ply (sportweight) yarn.

Size
64cm (25¼in) from the tip of the nose to the end of the back leg

Note
This dog is knitted using a double strand of yarn throughout, except for the nose.

Head
Cast on 14 sts using a double strand of brown 5-ply (sportweight) yarn and 4.5mm (UK 7, US 7) knitting needles and purl 1 row.

Next row: K1, M1, K to last st, M1, K1 [16 sts].
Next row: P1, M1, P to last st, M1, P1 [18 sts].
Rep last two rows twice more [26 sts].
Next row: K1, M1, K to last st, M1, K1 [28 sts].
Purl 1 row.
Rep last two rows twice more [32 sts].
Next row: K15, M1, K2, M1, K15 [34 sts].
Next row: P16, M1, P2, M1, P16 [36 sts].
Next row: K17, M1, K2, M1, K17 [38 sts].
Next row: P18, M1, P2, M1, P18 [40 sts].
Next row: K19, M1, K2, M1, K19 [42 sts].
Next row: P20, M1, P2, M1, P20 [44 sts].
Next row: K21, M1, K2, M1, K21 [46 sts].
Purl 1 row.
Next row: K22, M1, K2, M1, K22 [48 sts].
Work 9 rows in SS.
Next row: K1, ssK, K18, ssK, K2, K2tog, K18, K2tog, K1 [44 sts].
Purl 1 row.
Next row: K1, ssK, K16, ssK, K2, K2tog, K16, K2tog, K1 [40 sts].
Purl 1 row.
Next row: K1, ssK, K14, ssK, K2, K2tog, K14, K2tog, K1 [36 sts].
Next row: P1, P2tog, P12, P2tog, P2, P2togtbl, P12, P2togtbl, P1 [32 sts].
Next row: K1, ssK, K10, ssK, K2, K2tog, K10, K2tog, K1 [28 sts].
Next row: P1, P2tog, P8, P2tog, P2, P2togtbl, P8, P2togtbl, P1 [24 sts].
Next row: K1, ssK, K6, ssK, K2, K2tog, K6, K2tog, K1 [20 sts].
Next row: P1, P2tog, P4, P2tog, P2, P2togtbl, P4, P2togtbl, P1 [16 sts].
Cast off using the three needle cast off technique (see page 13).

Body, front legs and tail

Start at the front legs as follows:

Left front leg

Cast on 11 sts using a double strand of brown 5-ply (sportweight) yarn and 4.5mm (UK 7, US 7) knitting needles, and purl 1 row.

Next row: K9, w&t.

Next row: P6, w&t.

Next row: K5, w&t.

P to end of row. *

Next row: Cast on 5 sts, K to end of row [16 sts].

Work 13 rows in SS.

Next row: Cast off 6 sts, K3, cast off 6 sts [4 sts].

Place rem 4 sts on a stitch holder.

Right front leg

Work as for left front leg to *.

Knit 1 row.

Next row: Cast on 5 sts, P to end of row [16 sts].

Work 12 rows in SS.

Next row: Cast off 6 sts, K3, cast off 6 sts [4 sts].

Place rem 4 sts on a stitch holder.

With RS facing knit across 4 sts of left front leg, turn work and cast on 32 sts, turn work and knit across 4 sts of right leg [40 sts].

Work 17 rows in SS.

Next row: K1, M1, K to last st, M1, K1 [42 sts].

Work 3 rows in SS.

Continue in SS, changing colour and working in stripe pattern as follows, using a double strand of each colour yarn:

Purple – Work 18 rows.

Turquoise – Work 16 rows.

Teal – Work 8 rows.

Light brown – Work 12 rows.

Bright green – Work 14 rows.

Red – Work 18 rows.

Finally, change back to brown 5-ply (sportweight) yarn and work a further 8 rows.

Next row: K1, ssK, K to last 3 sts, K2tog, K1 [40 sts].

Work 3 rows in SS.

Next row: K1, ssK, K to last 3 sts, K2tog, K1 [38 sts].

Purl 1 row.

Rep last two rows once more [36 sts].

Next row: K1, ssK, K14, M1, K2, M1, K14, K2tog, K1 [36 sts].

Next row: P17, M1, P2, M1, P17 [38 sts].

Next row: K1, ssK, K15, M1, K2, M1, K15, K2tog, K1 [38 sts].

Next row: P1, P2tog, P15, M1, P2, M1, P15, P2togtbl, P1 [38 sts].

Next row: Cast off 13 sts, K4, M1, K2, M1, K to last 3 sts, K2tog, K1 [26 sts].

Next row: Cast off 13 sts, P to last 3 sts, P2togtbl, P1 [12 sts].

Next row: K1, ssK, K2, M1, K2, M1, K2, K2tog, K1 [12 sts].

Next row: P1, P2tog, P2, M1, P2, M1, P2, P2togtbl, P1 [12 sts].

Next row: K1, ssK, K to last 3 sts, K2tog, K1 [10 sts].

Next row: P1, P2tog, P4, P2togtbl, P1 [8 sts].

Next row: (K2tog) four times [4 sts].

Thread yarn through rem sts and fasten.

Bottom gusset

Cast on 8 sts using a double strand of brown 5-ply (sportweight) yarn and 4.5mm (UK 7, US 7) knitting needles. Starting with a knit row, work 2 rows in SS.

Next row: K1, M1, K to last st, M1, K1 [10 sts].

Next row: P1, M1, P to last st, M1, P1 [12 sts].

Rep last two rows once more [16 sts].

Work 2 rows in SS.

Next row: K1, M1, K to last st, M1, K1 [18 sts].
Work 25 rows in SS.
Next row: K1, M1, K to last st, M1, K1 [20 sts].
Work 95 rows in SS.
Next row: K1, ssK, K to last 3 sts, K2tog, K1 [18 sts].
Work 11 rows in SS.
Next row: K1, ssK, K to last 3 sts, K2tog, K1 [16 sts].
Purl 1 row.
Rep the last two rows four more times [8 sts].
Work 4 rows in SS.
Next row: K1, ssK, K to last 3 sts, K2tog, K1 [6 sts].
Work 3 rows in SS.
Rep last four rows once more [4 sts].
Next row: (K2tog) twice [2 sts].
Next row: P2tog.
Fasten off rem st.

Nose

Cast on 10 sts using black 4-ply (fingering) yarn and
2.75mm (UK 12, US 2) knitting needles and, starting
with a knit row, work 2 rows in SS.
Next row: K7, w&t.
Next row: P4, w&t.
Next row: K to end of row.
Purl 1 row.

Nothing beats
a good sleep.

Next row: K3, ssK, K2tog, K3 [8 sts].
Purl 1 row.
Next row: K2, ssK, K2tog, K2 [6 sts].
Purl 1 row.
Next row: K1, ssK, K2tog, K1 [4 sts].
Purl 1 row.
Thread yarn through rem sts and fasten, leaving a length of yarn to use to embroider the mouth.

Ears (make two)
Cast on 11 sts using a double strand of brown 5-ply (sportweight) yarn and 4.5mm (UK 7, US 7) knitting needle. Starting with a knit row, work 6 rows in SS.
Next row: K1, M1, K to last st, M1, K1 [13 sts].
Work 3 rows in SS.
Next row: K1, M1, K to last st, M1, K1 [15 sts].
Work 9 rows in SS.
Next row: K1, ssK, K to last 3 sts, K2tog, K1 [13 sts].
Purl 1 row.
Rep last two rows twice more [9 sts].
Cast off.

Ear linings (make two)
Each ear lining is knitted using a different shade. I chose teal and purple.
Cast on 9 sts using a double strand of 5-ply (sportweight) yarn in the colour of your choice and 4.5mm (UK 7, US 7) knitting needles. Starting with a knit row, work 4 rows in SS.
Next row: K1, M1, K to last st, M1, K1 [11 sts].
Work 3 rows in SS.
Next row: K1, M1, K to last st, M1, K1 [13 sts].
Work 7 rows in SS.
Next row: K1, ssK, K to last 3 sts, K2tog, K1 [11 sts].
Next row: P1, P2tog, P to last 3 sts, P2togtbl, P1 [9 sts].
Next row: K1, ssK, K to last 3 sts, K2tog, K1 [7 sts].
Cast off.

Back legs (make two)
Cast on 11 sts using a double strand of brown 5-ply (sportweight) yarn and 4.5mm (UK 7, US 7) knitting needles and purl 1 row.
Next row: K9, w&t.
Next row: P6, w&t.
Next row: K5, w&t.
P to end of row.
Next row: Cast on 5 sts, K to end of row [16 sts].
Work 12 rows in SS.
Cast off.

Collar
Cast on 7 sts using a double strand of red 5-ply (sportweight) yarn and 4.5mm (UK 7, US 7) knitting needles and work in SS until collar is long enough to go around the dog's neck. Cast off.

Making up
Pin and sew one front leg seam, folding the shapings to make the foot and stuff with toy filling. Repeat for second front leg.

Pin the bottom gusset on to the body, matching the cast-off end of the gusset (thinner end) to the tail of the dog. Sew the gusset in place, stuffing firmly with toy filling as you go.

Fold the front legs over on to the gusset, making sure they will lie flat and sew in place using the picture as guidance.

Pin and sew the back leg seam, folding the shapings to make the foot and stuff with toy filling. Repeat for second back leg.

Sew the two legs to the back of the dog, using the picture for guidance and placing at the same level as the front legs.

Placing the cast-off edge at the back of the head, sew the seam that will go underneath the head, stuffing with toy filling as you go. Sew the cast-on edges together up to the nose. To finish the head, see page 13 for instructions on how to gather the nose.

Pin the black-shanked buttons in place as eyes, using the pictures for guidance. Sew in place. Run the yarn from the back of the eye down to the base of the head and pull slightly, secure. Repeat for the second eye. This gives the eyes a much more realistic look.

With WS together, pin one ear to one ear lining and carefully sew the seam around the ear. Repeat for second ear. Pin the ears in place on the top of the head, using the picture for guidance. Sew in place.

Sew the nose to the front of the face and embroider on the mouth, using the length of yarn left at the end of the nose and straight stitches.

Firmly sew the head to the body. Sew the cast-on and cast-off edges of the collar together and place around the dog's neck.

Fluffy Floppy Dog

Everyone loves Fluffy, because his silky fur is super soft and cuddly. His body and legs are knitted in one piece, making him an easy project to sew together.

Materials
- 75m (82yd) of faux fur yarn
- 20m (22yd) of grey 5-ply (sportweight) yarn
- Small amount of black 4-ply (fingering) yarn
- Small amount of blue 5-ply (sportweight) yarn
- Two 16mm (⅝in) black buttons for eyes
- Toy filling

Needles
- 4.5mm (UK 7, US 7) knitting needles
- 2.75mm (UK 12, US 2) knitting needles
- 3.25mm (UK 10, US 3) knitting needles

Tension
15–16 sts worked in SS using 4.5mm (UK 7, US 7) knitting needles and faux fur yarn; measured over 10cm (4in)

Size
25cm (10in) from nose to tail

Note
This dog is knitted in SS. When you sew him together, place the WS on the outside as this is the fluffier side.

Body and legs (made in one piece)
Cast on 42 sts using fur yarn and 4.5mm (UK 7, US 7) knitting needles.
Starting with a purl row, work 3 rows in SS.
Next row: K1, M1, K to last st, M1, K1 [44 sts].
Work 3 rows in SS.

Next row: K1, K2tog, K to last 3 sts, K2tog, K1 [42 sts].
Work 3 rows in SS.
Cast off 12 sts at the beg of the next two rows [18 sts].
Starting with a knit row, work 16 rows in SS.
Cast on 12 sts at the beg of the next two rows [42 sts].
Starting with a knit row, work 3 rows in SS.
Next row: P1, M1, P to last st, M1, P1 [44 sts].
Work 3 rows in SS.
Next row: P1, P2tog, P to last 3 sts, P2tog, P1 [42 sts].
Work 6 rows in SS.
Next row: K1, M1, K to last st, M1, K1 [44 sts].
Work 3 rows in SS.
Next row: K1, K2tog, K to last 3 sts, K2tog, K1 [42 sts].
Work 3 rows in SS.
Cast off 12 sts at the beg of the next two rows [18 sts].
Next row: K1, M1, K to last st, M1, K1 [20 sts].
Work 14 rows in SS.
Next row: P1, P2tog, P to last 3 sts, P2tog, P1 [18 sts].
Cast on 12 sts at the beg of the next two rows [42 sts].
Starting with a knit row, work 3 rows in SS.
Next row: P1, M1, P to last st, M1, P1 [44 sts].
Work 3 rows in SS.
Next row: P1, P2tog, P to last 3 sts, P2tog, P1 [42 sts].
Work 3 rows in SS.
Cast off.

Head

Cast on 12 sts using fur yarn and 4.5mm (UK 7, US 7) knitting needles.

Next row: (Kfb) twelve times [24 sts].

Starting with a purl row, work 13 rows in SS.

Next row: K8, (Kfb) eight times, K8 [32 sts].

Purl 1 row.

Next row: K8, (Kfb) sixteen times, K8 [48 sts].

Work 5 rows in SS.

Next row: K8, (K2tog) sixteen times, K8 [32 sts].

Purl 1 row.

Cast off using the three needle cast off technique (see page 13).

Nose

Cast on 5 sts using black 4-ply (fingering) yarn and 2.75mm (UK 12, US 2) knitting needles.

Purl 1 row.

Next row: K1, M1, K to last st, M1, K1 [7 sts].

Purl 1 row.

Rep last two rows once more [9 sts].

Work 4 rows in SS.

Next row: K1, ssK, K to last 3 sts, K2tog, K1 [7 sts].

Purl 1 row.

Rep last two rows once more [5 sts].

Cast off.

Outer ears (make two)

Using fur yarn and 4.5mm (UK 7, US 7) knitting needles, cast on 8 sts and, starting with a knit row, work 4 rows in SS.

Next row: K1, M1, K to last st, M1, K1 [10 sts].

Work 5 rows in SS.

Rep last six rows once more [12 sts].

Next row: K1, K2tog, K to last 3 sts, K2tog, K1 [10 sts].

Purl 1 row.

Work last two rows once more [8 sts].

Cast off.

Ear linings (make two)

Using grey 5-ply (sportweight) yarn and 3.25mm (UK 10, US 3) knitting needles, cast on 8 sts and, starting with a knit row, work 6 rows in SS.

Next row: K1, M1, K to last st, M1, K1 [10 sts].
Work 7 rows in SS.
Rep last eight rows once more [12 sts].
Next row: K1, ssK, K to last 3 sts, K2tog, K1 [10 sts].
Purl 1 row.
Next row: K1, ssK, K to last 3 sts, K2tog, K1 [8 sts].
Next row: P1, P2tog, P to last 3 sts, P2togtbl, P1 [6 sts].
Cast off.

Tail

Using fur yarn and 4.5mm (UK 7, US 7) knitting needles, cast on 10 sts and, starting with a knit row, work 6 rows in SS.
Next row: K1, M1, K3, M1, K2, M1, K3, M1, K1 [14 sts].
Work 5 rows in SS.
Next row: (K2tog) seven times [7 sts].
Thread yarn through rem sts and sew closed, sew side seam of tail.

Making up

With the WS on the outside, slightly gather the cast-on end of the head and sew together: this forms the front of the face. Sew the seam that forms the bottom of the head, stuffing with toy filling as you go. The cast-off edge forms the back of the head.

Slightly gather the nose and sew to the front top edge of the face, placing a small amount of toy filling inside. Sew the black buttons in place as eyes using the pictures as guidance.

Pin one ear lining piece to one outer ear piece making sure that the RS of the ear lining piece and the WS (fluffier side) of the ear piece face outwards. Carefully sew the lining to the outer ear. Repeat for the second ear. Pin both completed ears in place on the head and sew on firmly.

To put the body together, fold it in half so that the cast-on and cast-off edges are together (use the diagram to the right for guidance). You can then see the finished shape of the dog's legs and body.

Sew up the side and leg seams of the body, stuffing lightly with toy filling as you go. When you stroke the body of the dog the 'pile' of the fur will go one way; the pile should go towards the back of the dog.

Sew the head firmly to the front of the body.

Place a small amount of toy filling in the end of the tail and sew it in place on the back of the dog using the picture as guidance.

Collar

Using blue 5-ply (sportweight) yarn and 3.25mm (UK 10, US 3) knitting needles, cast on 6 sts and work in SS until the collar fits around the neck. Cast off.

Place the collar around the dog's neck and sew the cast-on and cast-off edges together.

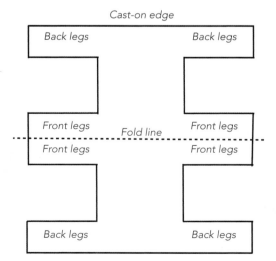

Circus Dogs

These playful characters fit into your hand perfectly and their cheerful expressions are enough to make anyone smile. With a small bag of weighting beads inside them, you can use them as little juggling dogs.

Materials
40m (43¾yd) of 5-ply (sportweight) yarn in orange, turquoise, citron and brown (this is enough to make all three dogs)
Stitch holders
Spare needle
Toy filling
Small fabric bag filled with weighting beads
Two 6mm (¼in) black beads
Black sewing cotton and sewing needle

Needles
3.25mm (UK 10, US 3) knitting needles

Tension
5 sts measured over 2cm (¾in) and worked in SS, using 3.25mm (UK 10, US 3) knitting needles and 5-ply (sportweight) yarn

Size
Approximately 8cm (3⅛in) tall

Note
You will need to choose one shade to use as the main colour (MC). The other two will be contrast colour 1 (CC1) and contrast colour 2 (CC2). The brown is used for the nose and ears.

Body, head and tail
Starting at the tail, cast on 4 sts using MC. Work 4 rows in SS, starting with a knit row.
Next row: K1, M1, K2, M1, K1 [6 sts].
Work 3 rows in SS.
Cast on 9 sts at the beginning of the next two rows [24 sts].

Next row: K1, M1, K to last st, M1, K1 [26 sts].
Purl 1 row.
Next row: K1, ssK, K7, K2tog, K2, ssK, K7, K2tog, K1 [22 sts].
Work 3 rows in SS.
Next row: K1, ssK, K5, K2tog, K2, ssK, K5, K2tog, K1 [18 sts].
Work 3 rows in SS.
Next row: K1, ssK, K3, K2tog, K2, ssK, K3, K2tog, K1 [14 sts].
Purl 1 row.
Next row: Cast off 4 sts, K5, cast off rem 4 sts [6 sts].
Place rem 6 sts on a stitch holder or spare needle.
Now work the two sides which form the bottom part of the head when sewn together, using MC.
* Cast on 8 sts and, starting with a P row, work 3 rows in SS. *
Place sts on a holder.
Rep from * to * in order to make the second section.
With RS facing, K1, M1, K across rem 7 sts, K across 6 sts from body and then K across first 7 sts of second head section on the holder, M1, K1 [24 sts].
Next row: P11, M1, P2, M1, P11 [26 sts].
Work 4 rows in SS.
Next row: K1, ssK, K6, K2tog, K4, ssK, K6, K2tog, K1 [22 sts].
Next row: P8, P2tog, P2, P2togtbl, P8 [20 sts].
Next row: Cast off 8 sts, K3, cast off rem 8 sts [4 sts].
With WS facing rejoin yarn to rem 4 sts and work 3 rows in SS.
Next row: K1, M1, K2, M1, K1 [6 sts].
Work 13 rows in SS.
Next row: K1, ssK, K2tog, K1 [4 sts].
Purl 1 row.
Cast off.

Drum roll, please!

Arms and legs (make four)

Cast on 4 sts using CC1 yarn and, starting with a knit row, work 4 rows in SS.

Next row: K1, K2tog, K1 [3 sts].

Next row: P1, M1, P2 [4 sts].

Work 4 rows in SS.

Cast off.

Nose

Cast on 3 sts using brown yarn and purl 1 row.

Next row: K1, M1, K to last st, M1, K1 [5 sts].

Purl 1 row.

Rep last two rows once more [7 sts].

Next row: K1, ssK, K1, K2tog, K1 [5 sts].

Purl 1 row.

Cast off.

Ears (make two)

Cast on 4 sts using brown yarn and, starting with a knit row, work 4 rows in SS.

Next row: K1, M1, K2, M1, K1 [6 sts].

Work 3 rows in SS.

Next row: K1, ssK, K2tog, K1 [4 sts].

Purl 1 row.

Cast off.

Ear linings (make two)

Cast on 3 sts using CC2 yarn and, starting with a knit row, work 4 rows in SS.

Next row: K1, M1, K1, M1, K1 [5 sts].

Work 3 rows in SS.

Front

Cast on 12 sts using CC1 yarn and work as follows:

Next row: K1, M1, K to last st, M1, K1 [14 sts].

Purl 1 row.

Next row: K1, ssK, K to last 3 sts, K2tog, K1 [12 sts].

Work 3 rows in SS.

Rep last four rows twice more [8 sts].

Next row: K1, ssK, K to last 3 sts, K2tog, K1 [6 sts].

Purl 1 row.

Cast off.

Base and tummy

Starting at the tail end, cast on 3 sts using CC2 yarn and purl 1 row.

Next row: K1, M1, K to last st, M1, K1 [5 sts].

Work 3 rows in SS.

Rep last four rows three more times [11 sts].

Next row: Cast off 3 sts, K4, cast off rem 3 sts [5 sts].

With WS facing rejoin yarn to rem 5 sts and P 1 row.

Next row: K1, M1, K to last st, M1, K1 [7 sts].

Work 5 rows in SS.

Next row: K1, ssK, K1, K2tog, K1 [5 sts].

Purl 1 row.

Next row: ssK, K1, K2tog [3 sts].

Cast off.

Next row: ssK, K1, K2tog [3 sts].
Purl 1 row.
Cast off.

Making up

Starting with the head, sew the bottom edge of each of the head sections together as shown. Sew the top gusset along the top edges of the head sections to form the top of the head. Sew the cast-off edge in place along the side flaps (see right). Stuff with toy filling. Sew the tail seam, then sew the front of the body in place along the side edges of the body, placing the cast-on edge at the bottom. Stuff gently, placing your small fabric bag inside the stuffing. Starting at the tail end, sew the base in place, folding the tummy up over the front of the dog and sewing it in place.

Sew each arm and leg in the same way: fold in half and sew up the seams. Sew each arm and leg in place, using the pictures for guidance. The legs are sewn either side of the tummy along the bottom seam and the arms a short way down the side seams.

Sew the ears and ear linings together, then sew the ears to the back of the seam created at the top of the head, using the picture for guidance.

Sew the nose in place as shown, placing the cast-off edge at the top, then sew the mouth using straight stitches.

Using black sewing cotton, sew the black beads in place for eyes using the picture for guidance.

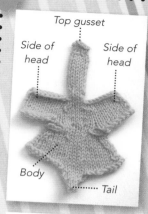

Top gusset
Side of head
Side of head
Body
Tail

Bottom seam of head

Sewing up the head

Upper left: *The body and head, ready to be sewn up.*

Upper right: *Stuff the piece after you sew the narrow central flap to the side flaps.*

Lower left: *The body pieces folded in, ready for the front to be sewn on.*

That didn't happen in rehearsal...

Black and White Terriers

If you are relatively new to knitting then have a go at these cute chaps. They are knitted in garter stitch (just knit) and every part of the dog is just a knitted rectangle. The only bit of shaping is on the ears to make them triangular. A super-easy, super-cute project!

Materials

36m (39⅜yd) of 8-ply (DK) eyelash yarn
Small amount of black 4-ply (fingering) yarn
Two 6mm (¼in) black beads for eyes
Toy filling
Chenille sticks
Small amount of tartan ribbon
Black sewing cotton and sewing needle

Needles

3.5mm (UK 9/10, US 4) knitting needles
2.75mm (UK 12, US 2) knitting needles

Tension

18 sts worked in GS using 3.5mm (UK 9/10, US 4) knitting needles and 8-ply (DK) eyelash yarn, and measured over 10cm (4in)

Size

14cm (5½in) from nose to tail, and 12cm (4¾in) from tip of ear to toe

Body

Cast on 26 sts using 8-ply (DK) eyelash yarn and 3.5mm (UK 9/10, US 4) knitting needles.
Work 8cm (3⅛in) in GS.
Cast off.

Legs (make four)

Cast on 8 sts using 8-ply (DK) eyelash yarn and 3.5mm (UK 9/10, US 4) knitting needles.
Work 4cm (1½in) in GS.
Thread yarn through sts and fasten.

Head

Cast on 10 sts using 8-ply (DK) eyelash yarn and 3.5mm (UK 9/10, US 4) knitting needles.
Work 15cm (6in) in GS.
Cast off.

Nose

Cast on 5 sts using black 4-ply (fingering) yarn and 2.75mm (UK 12, US 2) knitting needles.
Work 5 rows in GS.
Cast off, leaving a length of yarn long enough to embroider the mouth.

Ears (make two)

Cast on 6 sts using 8-ply (DK) eyelash yarn and 3.5mm (UK 9/10, US 4) knitting needles.
Work 6 rows in GS.
Next row: K2tog, K2, K2tog [4 sts].
Work 2 rows in GS.
Next row: K2tog, K2tog [2 sts].
Next row: K2tog and fasten off rem st.

Tail

Cast on 6 sts using 8-ply (DK) eyelash yarn and 3.5mm (UK 9/10, US 4) knitting needles.
Work 3cm (1⅛in) in GS.
Thread yarn through sts and gather. Fasten off yarn and sew side seam of tail.

Making up

The head is made from one long knitted rectangle which is folded to form the head shape. Start by folding the cast-on or cast-off edge as shown by fold line 1 on the diagram opposite. Sew the side seams this creates and stuff this section with toy filling. Fold the rest of the head over (fold line 2) and sew the other cast-on/off end to the stuffed head section you have made. You will now have a seam to sew for the back of the head, on either side, which runs from the top of the bottom of the head. Sew one side seam, stuff with toy filling and sew the second seam closed.

Sew the black beads in place as eyes, using the pictures for guidance, then sew the nose to the front of the face, folding the corners under to give a rounded look. Embroider the mouth using the black yarn. Sew the ends of yarn in on the ears and sew both ears on to the top of the head.

Fold the body in half and sew the cast on-edge together, then sew up the side seam, stuffing with toy filling as you go. Sew the cast-off edge together to form the back of the dog. Placing the seam underneath, sew the head to the body.

Sew the side seam of one leg and place a small amount of toy filling inside. Slide a chenille stick inside the leg and slide the chenille stick up inside the body of the dog, using the picture to guide you where to place the leg. Sew the leg to the body, then repeat for other three legs. Sew the tail to the back of the body. You do not need to stuff the tail, but if you wish you can place a small length of chenille stick inside it.

Finally, sew a length of tartan ribbon around the dog's neck as a collar. If necessary, use some sharp scissors to trim some of the longer hairs around the eyes to help them show more.

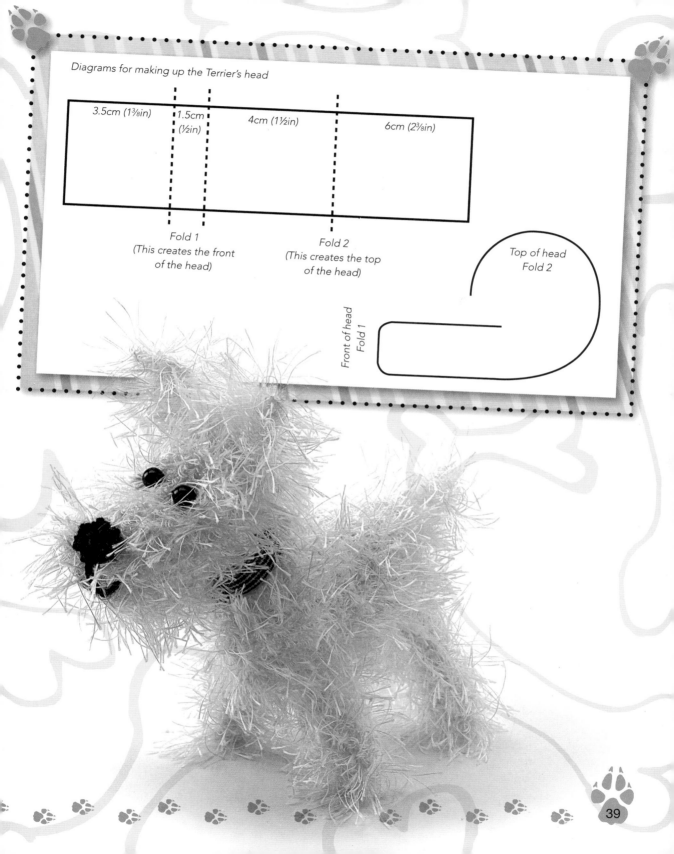

Diagrams for making up the Terrier's head

| 3.5cm (1⅜in) | 1.5cm (½in) | 4cm (1½in) | 6cm (2⅜in) |

Fold 1
(This creates the front
of the head)

Fold 2
(This creates the top
of the head)

Top of head
Fold 2

Front of head
Fold 1

Chic Chihuahua

This young lady has such an appealing expression that you will just want to make her. She is knitted using double knitting yarn and even has a smart diamante collar and a bag to be carried around in so she does not get her delicate feet dirty.

Materials
45m (49¼yd) of cream 8-ply (double knitting) yarn
60m (66yd) of beige 8-ply (double knitting) yarn
Small amounts of 4-ply (fingering) yarn in cream, black and fuchsia pink
Toy filling
Two 12mm (½in) black shanked buttons
10cm (4in) of rhinestone trim
Black sewing cotton and sewing needle
Safety pin
Two stitch markers
Chenille sticks

Needles
2.75mm (UK 12, US 2) knitting needles
3.75mm (UK 9, US 5) knitting needles

Tension
20–22 sts measured over 10cm (4in) and worked in SS using 3.75mm (UK 9, US 5) knitting needles and 8-ply (double knitting) yarn

Size
16cm (6¼in) from nose to tail, and 16cm (6¼in) from the top of the head to the bottom of the feet

Body and front legs
Start at bottom edge of right foot.
Using cream 8-ply (double knitting) yarn and 3.75mm (UK 9, US 5) knitting needles, cast on 10 sts.
* **Next row:** K5, turn.
Next row: P3, turn.
Next row: K3, turn.
Next row: P3, turn.
Next row: Knit to end of row.
Next row: P5, P3B, P2. *

Work 12 rows in SS.
Next row: Cast off 5 sts, K to end of row [5 sts].
Next row: Cast off 2 sts, P to end of row [3 sts].
Change to beige 8-ply (double knitting) yarn.
Next row: K1, M1, K to end of row [4 sts].
Next row: Cast on 12 sts, P to last st, M1, P1 [17 sts].
Knit 1 row.
Next row: Cast on 4 sts and P to end of row [21 sts].
Next row: K1, M1, K to last st, M1, K1 [23 sts].
Work 25 rows in SS, placing a stitch marker at either end of row 13.
Next row: K1, ssK, K to last 3 sts, K2tog, K1 [21 sts].
Next row: Cast off 4 sts, P to end of row [17 sts].
Knit 1 row.
Next row: Cast off 12 sts, P to last 3 sts, P2togtbl, P1 [4 sts].
Next row: K1, K2tog, K1 [3 sts].
Change to cream 8-ply (double knitting) yarn.
Next row: Cast on 2 sts, P to end of row [5 sts].
Next row: Cast on 5 sts, K to end of row [10 sts].
Work 13 rows in SS.
Work from * to * as for right foot.
Cast off.

Belly
Using cream 8-ply (double knitting) yarn and 3.75mm (UK 9, US 5) knitting needles, cast on 5 sts and, starting with a knit row, work 6 rows in SS.
Next row: K1, M1, K3, M1, K1 [7 sts].
Work 5 rows in SS.
Next row: K1, M1, K5, M1, K1 [9 sts].
Work 11 rows in SS.
Next row: K1, ssK, K3, K2tog, K1 [7 sts].
Work 15 rows in SS.
Next row: K1, ssK, K1, K2tog, K1 [5 sts].
Work 5 rows in SS.
Cast off.

Head

Using beige 8-ply (double knitting) yarn and 3.75mm (UK 9, US 5) knitting needles, cast on 14 sts and purl 1 row.

Next row: K1, M1, K to last st, M1, K1 [16 sts].
Next row: P1, M1, P to last st, M1, P1 [18 sts].
Rep last two rows once more [22 sts].
Next row: K6, M1, (K2, M1) twice, (K1, M1) twice, (K2, M1) twice, K6 [29 sts].
Work 3 rows in SS.
Next row: K8, M1, (K2, M1) three times, K1, (M1, K2) three times, M1, K8 [37 sts].
Work 3 rows in SS.
Next row: K10, (M1, K2) four times, M1, K1, (M1, K2) four times, M1, K10 [47 sts].
Work 3 rows in SS.
Next row: K1, ssK, K17, ssK, K3, K2tog, K17, K2tog, K1 [43 sts].
Purl 1 row.
Next row: K1, ssK, K15, ssK, K3, K2tog, K15, K2tog, K1 [39 sts].
Purl 1 row.
Next row: K1, ssK, K13, ssK, K3, K2tog, K13, K2tog, K1 [35 sts].
Next row: P1, P2tog, P to last 3 sts, P2togtbl, P1 [33 sts].
Cast off 13 sts at the beginning of the next two rows [7 sts].
Work 12 rows in SS.
Next row: K1, ssK, K1, K2tog, K1 [5 sts].
Purl 1 row.
Cast off.

Snout

Using cream 8-ply (double knitting) yarn and 3.75mm (UK 9, US 5) needles, cast on 14 sts and purl 1 row.
Next row: K1, M1, K to last st, M1, K1 [16 sts].
Next row: P1, M1, P to last st, M1, P1 [18 sts].
Rep last two rows once more [22 sts].
Work 2 rows in SS.
Cast off 9 sts at the beginning of the next two rows [4 sts].
Next row: (K2tog) twice [2 sts].
Purl 1 row.
Next row: K1, M1, K1 [3 sts].
Work 5 rows in SS.
Next row: Sl1, K2tog, psso [1 st].
Fasten off rem st.

Back leg (right)

Using cream 8-ply (double knitting) yarn and 3.75mm (UK 9, US 5) knitting needles, cast on 10 sts.
Next row: K5, turn.
Next row: P3, turn.
Next row: K3, turn.
Next row: P3, turn.
Next row: K to end of row.
Next row: P5, P3B, P2.
Work 12 rows in SS.
Next row: Cast off 5 sts, K to end of row [5 sts].
Next row: Cast off 1 st, P to end of row [4 sts].
Change to beige 8-ply (double knitting) yarn.
* **Next row:** K1, M1, K to last st, M1, K1 [6 sts].
Next row: P1, M1, P to last st, M1, P1 [8 sts].
Rep last two rows once more [12 sts].
Work 6 rows in SS.
Next row: K1, ssK, K to last three sts, K2tog, K1 [10 sts].
Next row: P1, P2tog, P to last 3 sts, P2togtbl, P1 [8 sts].
Next row: K1, ssK, K to last three sts, K2tog, K1 [6 sts].
Cast off.

Back leg (left)

Using cream 8-ply (double knitting) yarn and 3.75mm (UK 9, US 5) knitting needles, cast on 10 sts.

Next row: K8, turn.

Next row: P3, turn.

Next row: K3, turn.

Next row: P3, turn.

Next row: K to end of row.

Next row: P2, P3B, P5.

Work 12 rows in SS.

Next row: Cast off 1 st, K to end of row [9 sts].

Next row: Cast off 5 sts, P to end of row [4 sts].

Change to beige 8-ply (double knitting) yarn.

Work as for back leg (right) from * to end.

Ears (make two)

Using beige 8-ply (double knitting) yarn and 3.75mm (UK 9, US 5) knitting needles, cast on 14 sts and, starting with a knit row, work 6 rows in SS.

Next row: K1, ssK, K to last 3 sts, K2tog, K1 [12 sts].

Work 3 rows in SS.

Next row: K1, ssK, K to last 3 sts, K2tog, K1 [10 sts].

Purl 1 row.

Rep last two rows once more [8 sts].

Next row: K1, ssK, K2, K2tog, K1 [6 sts].

Next row: P1, P2tog, P2togtbl, P1 [4 sts].

Next row: (K2tog) twice [2 sts].

Next row: P2tog [1 st]. Fasten off rem st.

Ear linings (make two)

Using cream 4-ply (fingering) yarn and 2.75mm (UK 12, US 2) knitting needles, cast on 14 sts and, starting with a knit row, work 6 rows in SS.

Next row: K1, ssK, K to last 3 sts, K2tog, K1 [12 sts].

Work 3 rows in SS.

Rep last four rows once more [10 sts].

Next row: K1, ssK, K to last 3 sts, K2tog, K1 [8 sts].

Purl 1 row.

Rep last two rows twice more [4 sts].

Next row: ssK, K2tog [2 sts].

Next row: P2tog [1 st]. Fasten off rem st.

Tail

Using beige 8-ply (double knitting) yarn and 3.75mm (UK 9, US 5) knitting needles, cast on 8 sts and, starting with a knit row, work 4 rows in SS.

Next row: K6, w&t.

Next row: P4, w&t.

Next row: K3, w&t.

Next row: P to end of row.

Work 4 rows in SS.

Next row: K1, ssK, K2, K2tog, K1 [6 sts].

Work 3 rows in SS.

Next row: K1, ssK, K2tog, K1 [4 sts].

Purl 1 row.

Thread yarn through rem sts and fasten.

Nose

Using black 4-ply (fingering) yarn and 2.75mm (UK 12, US 2) knitting needles, cast on 5 sts. Starting with a knit row, work 4 rows in SS.

Next row: ssK, K1, K2tog [3 sts].

Next row: Sl1, P2tog, psso [1 st].

Thread yarn through rem st to fasten.

Making up

Starting with one of the front legs, thread a length of yarn through the bottom edge of the foot and gather to form the bottom of the foot. Sew the side seam and stuff with toy filling, placing a chenille stick inside the toy filling. Repeat for the second front leg.

Matching the middle of the cast-off edge of the belly to the stitch marker at the back of the body, and the middle of the cast-on edge of the belly to the stitch marker at the front of the body, pin the belly in place. Stuff the body firmly with toy filling, sewing the seams of the belly in place. Sew the cast-off edge of the top of each front leg to the belly.

Sew each back leg in the same way as the front legs. Pin the top of each back leg to the body as shown in the pictures, stuff gently with toy filling and sew in place, sewing the cast-off edge of the top of the leg to the belly. Push one end of the chenille stick from the leg into the body.

Sew the gusset at the back of the head (using the picture to the right as guidance), stuffing the head with toy filling as you work. Starting at the cast on edge, sew the seam on the snout and pin to the front of the face, stuffing with toy filling as you go The seam goes underneath the head. Sew in place and sew cream stripe up the centre of the head as shown.

With WS together, sew one ear lining to one ear. Repeat for the second ear. Pin the ears in place using the picture as guidance and then sew in place. Using black sewing cotton, sew the two black shanked buttons in place for eyes. Sew the black nose to the front of the head using black 4-ply (fingering) yarn. Sew the head firmly to the front of the body. The head will be a bit wobbly but the collar will stabilise it once it is sewn on.

Fold the tail in half and sew the side seam, stuffing the cast-on end with toy filling. Sew in place, using the pictures for guidance.

Chihauhua's doggy bag

Materials
75m (82yd) of sparkly pink 8-ply (double knitting) cotton yarn
Small amount of fuchsia pink 4-ply (fingering) yarn

Needles
3.5mm (UK 9/10, US 4) knitting needles
2.75mm (UK 12, US 2) knitting needles

Tension
24 sts measured over 10cm (4in) using 3.5mm (UK 9/10, US 4) knitting needles and 8-ply (double knitting) yarn

Bag
Starting with the base, cast on 24 sts using 3.5mm (UK 9/10, US 4) knitting needles and sparkly pink 8-ply (double knitting) yarn.
Work 7cm (2¾in) in GS.
Next row: Cast on 52 sts, K to end of row [76 sts].
Starting with a WS row, work 6cm (2⅜in) in SS ending with a WS row.
Next row: Cast off 17 sts, K to the end of the row [59 sts].
Next row: Cast off 3 sts, P to the end of the row [56 sts].
Cast off 2 sts at the beg of the next two rows [52 sts].
Rep last two rows once more [48 sts].
Work 2 rows in SS.
Cast off.

Collar
Using fuchsia pink 4-ply (fingering) yarn and 2.75mm (UK 12, US 2) knitting needles, cast on 5 sts and work in SS until the collar fits snugly around dog's neck. Cast off.

Place the collar around the dog's neck and sew the cast-on and cast-off edges together. Sew the rhinestone trim in place.

Top of bag

Cast on 5 sts using 3.5mm (UK 9/10, US 4) knitting needles and sparkly pink 8-ply (double knitting) yarn, and work in SS until the strip is long enough to go all around the top edge of the bag when slightly stretched. Cast off.

Note: This can alternatively be knitted as an i-cord (see page 12).

Handles (make two)

Cast on 5 sts using 3.5mm (UK 9/10, US 4) knitting needles and sparkly pink 8-ply (double knitting) yarn and work in SS until handle measures 11cm (4⅜in). Cast off.

Note: These can alternatively be knitted as an i-cord (see page 12).

Paw prints (make two)

Using fuchsia pink 4-ply (fingering) yarn and 2.75mm (UK 12, US 2) knitting needles, cast on 5 sts and purl 1 row.
Next row: K1, M1, K to last st, M1, K1 [7 sts].
Purl 1 row.
Cast off 2 sts at beg of the next two rows [3 sts].
Work 2 rows in SS.
Next row: Sl1, K2tog, psso [1 st].
Fasten off rem st.

Making up

Lay your knitted bag out and sew the two edges marked 1 to each other. Repeat for 2, 3 and 4 to make the bag shape. Pin the bag edging in place along the top shaped edge of the bag, covering the cast-off edge. Sew in place.

Pin the handles in place (see picture for guidance) and sew securely to the inside edge of the bag. Using fuchsia pink yarn, sew one paw print to one side of the bag and embroider four French knots (see page 12) as pads, using the picture for guidance on placement. Repeat with the second paw on the other side of the bag.

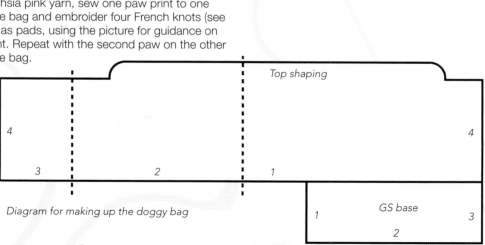

Diagram for making up the doggy bag

Mischief-makers

The cute little pups are irresistible. Made using a fluffy yarn they are easy to knit and quick to make, so why not have a whole litter?

Materials
60m (66yd) grey fluffy 10-ply (Aran) yarn
Small amount of black 4-ply (fingering) yarn
Two 8mm (⅜in) black shanked buttons

Needles
5mm (UK 6, US 8) knitting needles
2.75mm (UK 12, US 2) knitting needles

Tension
8–9 sts measured in SS over 5cm (2in) using grey fluffy 10-ply (Aran) yarn and 5mm (UK 12, US 2) knitting needles

Size
26cm (10¼in) from top of head to bottom of feet

Note
Each pup is knitted in SS but sewn together with the WS on the outside to give a fluffier appearance. The yarn listed above is sufficient to make one of the dogs – simply double the amount to make sure you have enough for his playmate.

Head
Using grey fluffy 10-ply (Aran) yarn and 5mm (UK 6, US 8) knitting needles, cast on 10 sts.
Next row: K2, M1, K1, M1, K4, M1, K1, M1, K2 [14 sts].
Next row: P3, M1, P1, M1, P6, M1, P1, M1, P3 [18 sts].
Next row: K4, M1, K1, M1, K8, M1, K1, M1, K4 [22 sts].
Purl 1 row.

Next row: K5, M1, K1, M1, K10, M1, K1, M1, K5 [26 sts].
Purl 1 row.
Next row: K6, M1, K1, M1, K12, M1, K1, M1, K6 [30 sts].
Work 3 rows in SS.
Next row: K5, ssK, K1, K2tog, K10, ssK, K1, K2tog, K5 [26 sts].
Purl 1 row.
Next row: K4, ssK, K1, K2tog, K8, ssK, K1, K2tog, K4 [22 sts].
Purl 1 row.
Next row: K3, ssK, K1, K2tog, K6, ssK, K1, K2tog, K3 [18 sts].
Work 3 rows in SS.
Cast off rem sts.

Legs (make two)
Using grey fluffy 10-ply (Aran) yarn and 5mm (UK 6, US 8) knitting needles, cast on 18 sts.
Next row: K8, M1, K2, M1, K8 [20 sts].
Work 3 rows in SS.
Next row: K7, K2tog, K2, ssK, K7 [18 sts].
Next row: P6, P2tog, P2, P2togtbl, P6 [16 sts].
Next row: K5, K2tog, K2, ssK, K5 [14 sts].
Next row: P4, P2tog, P2, P2togtbl, P4 [12 sts].
Work 12 rows in SS.
Cast off.

Arms (make two)
Using grey fluffy 10-ply (Aran) yarn and 5mm (UK 6, US 8) knitting needles, cast on 8 sts.
Next row: K1, M1, (K2, M1) three times, K1 [12 sts].
Work 5 rows in SS.
Next row: K2, K2tog, K4, K2tog, K2 [10 sts].
Work 11 rows in SS.
Cast off.

Ears (make four)

Using grey fluffy 10-ply (Aran) yarn and 5mm (UK 6, US 8) knitting needles, cast on 4 sts and purl 1 row.

Next row: K1, M1, K2, M1, K1 [6 sts].
Next row: P1, M1, P4, M1, P1 [8 sts].
Work 2 rows in SS.
Next row: K1, K2tog, K2, K2tog, K1 [6 sts].
Work 3 rows in SS.
Next row: K1, (K2tog) twice, K1 [4 sts].
Purl 1 row.
Cast off rem sts.

Nose

Using black 4-ply (fingering) yarn and 2.75mm (UK 12, US 2) knitting needles, cast on 3 sts and purl 1 row.

Next row: (K1, M1) twice, K1 [5 sts].
Work 2 rows in SS.
Next row: P2tog, P1, P2togtbl [3 sts].
Knit 1 row.
Cast off, leaving a length of yarn long enough to embroider the mouth.

Body

Using grey fluffy 10-ply (Aran) yarn and 5mm (UK 6, US 8) knitting needles, cast on 12 sts.

Next row: K3, Kfb, K4, Kfb, K3 [14 sts].
Next row: P3, Kfb, P6, Kfb, P3 [16 sts].
Next row: K4, Kfb, K6, Kfb, K4 [18 sts].
Next row: P4, Kfb, P8, Kfb, P4 [20 sts].
Next row: K5, Kfb, K8, Kfb, K5 [22 sts].
Next row: P5, Kfb, P10, Kfb, P5 [24 sts].
Next row: K6, Kfb, K10, Kfb, K6 [26 sts].
Next row: P6, Kfb, P12, Kfb, P6 [28 sts].
Next row: K7, Kfb, K12, Kfb, K7 [30 sts].
Next row: P7, Kfb, P14, Kfb, P7 [32 sts].
Knit 1 row.
Next row: P8, Kfb, P14, Kfb, P8 [34 sts].
Knit 1 row.
Next row: P8, Kfb, P16, Kfb, P8 [36 sts].
Work 4 rows in SS.
Next row: K8, ssK, K16, K2tog, K8 [34 sts].
Purl 1 row.

Next row: K8, ssK, K14, K2tog, K8 [32 sts].
Purl 1 row.
Next row: K7, ssK, K14, K2tog, K7 [30 sts].
Purl 1 row.
Next row: K7, ssK, K12, K2tog, K7 [28 sts].
Purl 1 row.
Next row: K6, ssK, K12, K2tog, K6 [26 sts].
Purl 1 row.
Next row: K6, ssK, K10, K2tog, K6 [24 sts].
Purl 1 row.
Next row: K5, ssK, K10, K2tog, K5 [22 sts].
Purl 1 row.
Next row: K5, ssK, K8, K2tog, K5 [20 sts].
Purl 1 row.
Next row: K4, ssK, K8, K2tog, K4 [18 sts].
Purl 1 row.
Next row: K4, ssK, K6, K2tog, K4 [16 sts].
Purl 1 row.
Next row: K3, ssK, K6, K2tog, K3 [14 sts].
Purl 1 row.
Cast off.

Tail
Using grey fluffy 10-ply (Aran) yarn and 5mm (UK 6, US 8) knitting needles, cast on 8 sts. Starting with a knit row, work 8 rows in SS.
Next row: K1, M1, (K2, M1) three times, K1 [12 sts].
Purl 1 row.
Next row: K1, K2tog, K1, (K2tog) twice, K1, K2tog, K1 [8 sts].
Cast off.

Making up
With the WS facing outwards and starting at the cast-on end of the body (bottom), sew up the back seam. Stuff with toy filling as you sew. Sew the cast-on edge together to form the bottom seam, ensuring the back seam is in the centre of the back. Sew the cast-off edge together to form the top seam.

With the WS facing outwards, sew up the back seam of the head. This seam will be underneath the head. Stuff with toy filling and sew the top and bottom seams as for the body.

Using black 4-ply (fingering) yarn, sew the nose in place and then sew on the black shanked buttons as eyes. Use the pictures for guidance on where to place them.

Attach grey fluffy 10-ply (Aran) yarn to the centre back of the head, then sew the head to the top edge of the body using the pictures for guidance.

With the WS facing outwards sew two ear pieces together. Repeat for the second ear. Sew the ears to the top of the head using the pictures for guidance and leaving approximately 1cm (⅜in) in between the ears.

With WS facing outwards, sew up the side seam of the arm. Stuff with toy filling and sew up the top and bottom seams. The cast-off end forms the top of the arm. Repeat for the second arm.

With the seam facing towards the back of the pup, sew the cast-off edge of the arm to the side of the body just under the head, using the pictures for guidance. Repeat for the second arm.

Sew up the back seam of the leg, stuff it with toy filling, then sew the foot closed. Sew up the top seam of the leg horizontally, so that the back seam is in the centre. Repeat for the second leg and sew the legs to the bottom of the body, towards the front of the pup. Sew up the side and bottom seams of the tail, but do not stuff it. Sew the top of the tail (cast-on end) to the back of the body. See pictures for guidance.

Bullseye

Bullseye has real character in his gleaming black eyes and just wants a hug. His black patches are knitted separately and sewn on after making him up; if you want to give him a few more patches you can easily make two or three more to sew on.

Materials
62m (68yd) of cream 10-ply (Aran) yarn
25m (27½yd) of black 10-ply (Aran) yarn
Toy filling
Two 10mm (⅜in) black shanked buttons
Black sewing cotton and sewing needle

Needles
4mm (UK 8, US 6) knitting needles

Tension
9–10 sts measured over 5cm (2in) and worked in SS using 4mm (UK 8, US 6) knitting needles and 10-ply (Aran) yarn

Size
Approximately 20cm (8in) tall when sitting down as shown opposite

Body front
Using cream 10-ply (Aran) yarn and 4mm (UK 8, US 6) knitting needles, cast on 20 sts and work 4 rows in SS, starting with a knit row.
Next row: K1, M1, K8, M1, K2, M1, K8, M1, K1 [24 sts].
Purl 1 row.
Next row: K1, M1, K10, M1, K2, M1, K10, M1, K1 [28 sts].
Purl 1 row.
Next row: K1, M1, K12, M1, K2, M1, K12, M1, K1 [32 sts].
Purl 1 row.
Next row: K1, M1, K14, M1, K2, M1, K14, M1, K1 [36 sts].
Work 15 rows in SS.
Next row: K1, ssK, K12, K2tog, K2, ssK, K12, K2tog, K1 [32 sts].
Work 3 rows in SS.
Next row: K1, ssK, K10, K2tog, K2, ssK, K10, K2tog, K1 [28 sts].
Purl 1 row.
Next row: K1, ssK, K8, K2tog, K2, ssK, K8, K2tog, K1 [24 sts].
Purl 1 row.
Next row: K1, ssK, K to last 3 sts, K2tog, K1 [22 sts].
Purl 1 row.
Rep last two rows three more times [16 sts].
Next row: K1, ssK, K2, K2tog, K2, ssK, K2, K2tog, K1 [12 sts].
Cast off (WS).

Body back

Using cream 10-ply (Aran) yarn and 4mm (UK 8, US 6) knitting needles, cast on 20 sts and work 2 rows in SS, starting with a knit row.

Next row: K1, M1, K8, M1, K2, M1, K8, M1, K1 [24 sts].

Purl 1 row.

Next row: K1, M1, K10, M1, K2, M1, K10, M1, K1 [28 sts].

Purl 1 row.

Next row: K1, M1, K12, M1, K2, M1, K12, M1, K1 [32 sts].

Work 15 rows in SS.

Next row: K1, ssK, K to last 3 sts, K2tog, K1 [30 sts].

Purl 1 row.

Rep last two rows eleven more times [8 sts].

Cast off.

Base

Using cream 10-ply (Aran) yarn and 4mm (UK 8, US 6) knitting needles, cast on 16 sts and, starting with a knit row, work 2 rows in SS.

Next row: K1, M1, K to last st, M1, K1 [18 sts].

Work 9 rows in SS.

Next row: K1, ssK, K to last 3 sts, K2tog, K1 [16 sts].

Purl 1 row.

Next row: K1, ssK, K to last 3 sts, K2tog, K1 [14 sts].

Next row: P1, P2tog, P to last 3 sts, P2togtbl, P1 [12 sts].

Cast off.

Legs (make two)

Using cream 10-ply (Aran) yarn and 4mm (UK 8, US 6) knitting needles, cast on 18 sts.

Next row: K8, M1, K2, M1, K8 [20 sts].

Work 3 rows in SS.

Next row: K9, M1, K2, M1, K9 [22 sts].

Work 3 rows in SS.

Next row: K10, M1, K2, M1, K10 [24 sts].

Purl 1 row.

Next row: K11, M1, K2, M1, K11 [26 sts].

Purl 1 row.

Next row: K12, M1, K2, M1, K12 [28 sts].

Purl 1 row.

Next row: K13, M1, K2, M1, K13 [30 sts].

Next row: P14, M1, P2, M1, P14 [32 sts].

Next row: K15, M1, K2, M1, K15 [34 sts].

Next row: P16, M1, P2, M1, P16 [36 sts].

Work 2 rows in SS.

Next row: K1, ssK, K12, K2tog, K2, K2tog, K12, ssK, K1 [32 sts].

Next row: P1, P2tog, P10, P2togtbl, P2, P2tog, P10, P2togtbl, P1 [28 sts].

Cast off 11 sts at the beginning of the next two rows [6 sts].

Work 2 rows in SS.

Next row: K1, M1, K to last st, M1, K1 [8 sts].

Purl 1 row.

Rep last two rows once more [10 sts].

Work 2 rows in SS.

Next row: K1, ssK, K to last 3 sts, K2tog, K1 [8 sts].

Purl 1 row.

Rep last two rows once more [6 sts].

Cast off.

Arms (make two)

Using cream 10-ply (Aran) yarn and 4mm (UK 8, US 6) needles, cast on 16 sts and, starting with a knit row, work 12 rows in SS.

Next row: K1, M1, K6, M1, K2, M1, K6, M1, K1 [20 sts].

Purl 1 row.

Next row: K1, M1, K8, M1, K2, M1, K8, M1, K1 [24 sts].

Work 3 rows in SS.

Next row: K1, ssK, K6, K2tog, K2, ssK, K6, K2tog, K1 [20 sts].

Next row: P1, P2tog, P4, P2togtbl, P2, P2tog, P4, P2togtbl, P1 [16 sts].

Cast off using the three needle cast off technique (see page 13).

Head

Using cream 10-ply (Aran) yarn and 4mm (UK 8, US 6) knitting needles, cast on 14 sts and purl 1 row.

Next row: K1, M1, K to last st, M1, K1 [16 sts].

Next row: P1, M1, P to last st, M1, P1 [18 sts].

Rep last two rows twice more [26 sts].

Next row: K1, M1, K to last st, M1, K1 [28 sts].

Purl 1 row.

Rep last two rows once more [30 sts].

Next row: K14, M1, K2, M1, K14 [32 sts].

Next row: P15, M1, P2, M1, P15 [34 sts].

Next row: K16, M1, K2, M1, K16 [36 sts].

Next row: P17, M1, P2, M1, P17 [38 sts].

Next row: K18, M1, K2, M1, K18 [40 sts].

Next row: P19, M1, P2, M1, P19 [42 sts].

Next row: K20, M1, K2, M1, K20 [44 sts].

Work 9 rows in SS.

Next row: K1, ssK, K16, K2tog, K2, ssK, K16, K2tog, K1 [40 sts].

Purl 1 row.

Next row: K1, ssK, K14, K2tog, K2, ssK, K14, K2tog, K1 [36 sts].

Purl 1 row.

Next row: K1, ssK, K12, K2tog, K2, ssK, K12, K2tog, K1 [32 sts].

Next row: P1, P2tog, P10, P2togtbl, P2, P2tog, P10, P2togtbl, P1 [28 sts].

Next row: K1, ssK, K8, K2tog, K2, ssK, K8, K2tog, K1 [24 sts].

Next row: P1, P2tog, P6, P2togtbl, P2, P2tog, P6, P2togtbl, P1 [20 sts].

Next row: K1, ssK, K4, K2tog, K2, ssK, K4, K2tog, K1 [16 sts].

Cast off using the three needle cast off technique (see page 13).

I've got a bone to pick with you...

Ears (make two in cream and two in black)

Using 10-ply (Aran) yarn and 4mm (UK 8, US 6) knitting needles, cast on 8 sts and, starting with a knit row, work 6 rows in SS.

Next row: K1, M1, K to last st, M1, K1 [10 sts].

Work 7 rows in SS.

Next row: K1, M1, K to last st, M1, K1 [12 sts].

Work 3 rows in SS.

Next row: K1, ssK, K to last 3 sts, K2tog, K1 [10 sts].

Next row: P1, P2tog, P to last 3 sts, P2togtbl, P1 [8 sts].

Cast off.

Nose

Using black 10-ply (Aran) yarn and 4mm (UK 8, US 6) knitting needles, cast on 5 sts and, starting with a knit row, work 4 rows in SS.

Next row: SsK, K1, K2tog [3 sts].

Purl 1 row.

Next row: Sl1, K2tog, psso [1 st].

Fasten off rem st, leaving a length of yarn long enough to embroider the mouth.

Patch on face

Using black 10-ply (Aran) yarn and 4mm (UK 8, US 6) knitting needles, cast on 4 sts and purl 1 row.

Next row: K1, M1, K2, M1, K1 [6 sts].

Next row: P1, M1, K4, M1, P1 [8 sts].

Work 2 rows in SS.

Next row: K1, ssK, K2, K2tog, K1 [6 sts].

Next row: P1, P2tog, P2togtbl, P1 [4 sts].

Cast off (RS).

Tail

Using black 10-ply (Aran) yarn and 4mm (UK 8, US 6) knitting needles, cast on 10 sts and, starting with a knit row, work 4 rows in SS.

* Next row: K8, w&t.

Next row: P6, w&t.

Next row: K to end of row.

Purl 1 row. *

Rep from * to * once more.

Next row: K1, ssK, K to last 3 sts, K2tog, K1 [8 sts].

Purl 1 row.

Rep last two rows once more [6 sts].

Next row: (K2tog) three times [3 sts].

Thread yarn through rem sts and fasten, leaving enough yarn to sew the side seam of the tail.

Patch on body

Using black 10-ply (Aran) yarn and 4mm (UK 8, US 6) knitting needles, cast on 7 sts and knit 1 row.

Next row: P1, M1, P to last st, M1, P1 [9 sts].

Work 2 rows in SS.

Next row: K1, M1, K to last st, M1, K1 [11 sts].

Work 3 rows in SS.

Next row: K1, ssK, K to last 3 sts, K2tog, K1 [9 sts].

Purl 1 row.

Rep last two rows once more [7 sts].

Cast off.

... I think you're trying to stitch me up!

Making up

Pin and sew the side seams of the body pieces together, placing the cast-on edges at the bottom. Stuff the body with toy filling, pin the base in place then sew the base to the body, placing the cast-on edge at the front.

With the head shaping forming the top of the head and the cast-off edge forming the back of the head, sew up the seam along the bottom of the head and up the front. When you get to the cast-on edges, run a length of cream 10-ply (Aran) yarn through a row of stitches a couple of stitches in from the cast-off edge and gather. This gives a rounder finish to the nose (see page 13).

Sew the black patch on to the face using the picture for guidance. Sew the black shanked buttons in place as eyes using black sewing cotton. Run the thread from the back of each eye down to the base of the head and pull slightly to secure. This gives the eyes a much more realistic look.

With the WS together, sew the two black ear pieces together. Repeat for the cream ear. Pin the ears in place on the top of the head, making sure that the black ear is on the opposite side of the head to the black eye patch. Sew in place.

Sew the nose to the front of the face, placing the cast-on edge at the top, and embroider the mouth using straight stitches and the length of black 10-ply (Aran) yarn left from the nose.

Sew up the side seam of the first arm and fold so that this seam is beneath the arm. Sew the cast-off stitches of the arm together, then stuff with toy filling and embroider the spaces between the fingers on the paw using black yarn and straight stitches. Repeat for the second arm, then pin the arms on the body and sew in place.

Sew up the back seam of the leg, stuff with toy filling and sew the base of the foot in place. Repeat for the second leg, then pin both in place so that the back of the leg is just above the base/body seam and the seam is underneath the leg. Use the picture for guidance when placing the legs.

Sew the black body patch in place. Sew up the seam of the tail (this will be at the top when it is sewn on to the body) and place a small amount of toy filling inside. Sew it in place at the bottom of the body using the pictures for guidance.

Stripes

Daredevil Stripes has a look of fun on his stripy face. Follow the colour sequence and you will end up with your very own colourful dog. Why not knit him in shades of blue for a baby boy? Just remember to use safety eyes in place of buttons.

Materials
70m (76½yd) of pink 10-ply (Aran) cotton yarn (MC)
62m (68yd) of purple 10-ply (Aran) cotton yarn (CC)
Small amount of black 4-ply (fingering) cotton yarn
Toy filling and chenille sticks

Needles
3.75mm (UK 9, US 5) knitting needles
2.75mm (UK 12, US 2) knitting needles

Tension
20 sts measured over 10cm (4in) and worked in SS using 3.75mm (UK 9, US 5) knitting needles and 10-ply (Aran) cotton yarn

Size
18cm (7in) tall when sitting down as pictured on page 58

Notes
Six row stripe pattern
Starting with a knit row and working in SS:
Work 2 rows in CC.
Work 4 rows in MC.

Four row stripe pattern
Starting with a knit row and working in SS:
Work 2 rows in CC.
Work 2 rows in MC.

Head
Cast on 10 sts using MC and 3.75mm (UK 9, US 5) knitting needles and purl 1 row.
Next row: K1, M1, K to last st, M1, K1 [12 sts].
Next row: P1, M1, P to last st, M1, P1 [14 sts].
Next row: K1, M1, K4, M1, K4, M1, K4, M1, K1 [18 sts].

Purl 1 row.
Next row: K1, M1, K5, M1, K6, M1, K5, M1, K1 [22 sts].
Purl 1 row.
Next row: K1, M1, K6, M1, K8, M1, K6, M1, K1 [26 sts].
Purl 1 row.
Next row: K1, M1, K7, M1, K10, M1, K7, M1, K1 [30 sts].
Purl 1 row.
Join in CC and work next 14 rows in the six row stripe pattern (see notes).
Next row: K12, M1, K6, M1, K12 [32 sts].
Next row: P13, M1, P6, M1, P13 [34 sts].
Next row: K14, M1, K6, M1, K14 [36 sts].
Purl 1 row.
Next row: K15, M1, K6, M1, K15 [38 sts].
Purl 1 row.
Next row: K16, M1, K6, M1, K16 [40 sts].
Work 7 rows in SS.
Continue in MC.
Work 2 rows in SS.
Next row: K1, ssK, K14, K2tog, K2, ssK, K14, K2tog, K1 [36 sts].
Purl 1 row.
Next row: K1, ssK, K12, K2tog, K2, ssK, K12, K2tog, K1 [32 sts].
Purl 1 row.
Next row: K1, ssK, K10, K2tog, K2, ssK, K10, K2tog, K1 [28 sts].
Next row: P1, P2tog, P8, P2togtbl, P2, P2tog, P8, P2togtbl, P1 [24 sts].
Next row: K1, ssK, K6, K2tog, K2, ssK, K6, K2tog, K1 [20 sts].
Next row: P1, P2tog, P4, P2togtbl, P2, P2tog, P4, P2togtbl, P1 [16 sts].
Cast off using the three needle cast off technique (see page 13).

Body (make two)

Cast on 10 sts using MC and 3.75mm (UK 9, US 5) knitting needles and, starting with a knit row, work 2 rows in SS.

The body is worked in the six row stripe pattern from now on.

Next row: K1, M1, K to last st, M1, K1 [12 sts].
Purl 1 row.

Rep last two rows four more times [20 sts].

Next row: K1, M1, K to last st, M1, K1 [22 sts].
Work 3 rows in SS.

Rep last four rows four more times [30 sts].
Work 6 rows in SS.

Next row: K1, ssK, K9, K2tog, K2, ssK, K9, K2tog, K1 [26 sts].
Purl 1 row.

Next row: K1, ssK, K7, K2tog, K2, ssK, K7, K2tog, K1 [22 sts].
Purl 1 row.

Next row: K1, ssK, K5, K2tog, K2, ssK, K5, K2tog, K1 [18 sts].

Next row: P1, P2tog, P3, P2togtbl, P2, P2tog, P3, P2togtbl, P1 [14 sts].

From now on, work only in MC.

Next row: K1, ssK, K1, K2tog, K2, ssK, K1, K2tog, K1 [10 sts].
Cast off.

Nose

Using black 4-ply (fingering) yarn and 2.75mm (UK 12, US 2) needles cast on 5 sts and purl 1 row.

Next row: K1, M1, K to last st, M1, K1 [7 sts].
Work 3 rows in SS.

Next row: K1, ssK, K1, K2tog, K1 [5 sts].
Purl 1 row.

Cast off, leaving a long enough length of yarn to embroider the mouth.

Ears (make two)

Using CC cast on 6 sts using 3.75mm (UK 9, US 5) knitting needles and, starting with a knit row, work 18 rows in SS.

Next row: K1, ssK, K2tog, K1 [4 sts].
Purl 1 row.

Next row: K1, M1, K2, M1, K1 [6 sts].
Work 18 rows in SS.
Cast off.

Arms (make two)

Using MC, cast on 12 sts using 3.75mm (UK 9, US 5) knitting needles and, starting with a knit row, work 2 rows in SS.

From now on work in the four row stripe pattern.

Work 12 rows in SS.

Continue in CC only.

Next row: K1, M1, K4, M1, K2, M1, K4, M1, K1 [16 sts].

Purl 1 row.

Next row: K1, M1, K6, M1, K2, M1, K6, M1, K1 [20 sts].

Work 5 rows in SS.

Next row: K1, ssK, K4, K2tog, K2, ssK, K4, K2tog, K1 [16 sts].

Next row: P1, P2tog, P2, P2togtbl, P2, P2tog, P2, P2togtbl, P1 [12 sts].

Cast off, using the three needle cast off technique (see page 13).

Tail

Using CC, cast on 10 sts using 3.75mm (UK 9, US 5) knitting needles and, starting with a knit row, work 10 rows in SS.

Next row: (K2tog) five times [5 sts].

Thread yarn through rem sts, gather and sew the side seam of the tail. Fasten off yarn.

Legs (make two)

Using CC cast on 14 sts using 3.75mm (UK 9, US 5) knitting needles and, starting with a knit row, work 16 rows in the four row stripe pattern.

Cast off.

Feet (make two)

Using CC cast on 8 sts using 3.75mm (UK 9, US 5) knitting needles and purl 1 row.

Next row: K1, M1, K to last st, M1, K1 [10 sts].

Next row: P1, M1, P to last st, M1, P1 [12 sts].

Work 6 rows in SS.

Next row: K1, ssK, K to last 3 sts, K2tog, K1 [10 sts].

Work 2 rows in SS.

Next row: P1, M1, P to last st, M1, P1 [12 sts].

Work 6 rows in SS.

Next row: K1, ssK, K to last 3 sts, K2tog, K1 [10 sts].

Next row: P1, P2tog, P to last 3 sts, P2togtbl, P1 [8 sts].

Knit 1 row.

Cast off.

Making up

Sew the side seams of the body with the cast-off end forming the base. Stuff with toy filling. Sew the head seam that forms the bottom and front of the head. Stuff the head with toy filling as you sew.

Slightly gather the nose and sew to the front top edge of the face, placing a small amount of toy filling inside. Using the length of yarn left from the nose, embroider the mouth using straight stitches. Using black 4-ply (fingering) cotton yarn, embroider two French knots (see page 12) for eyes just behind the first purple stripe.

Fold one ear in half lengthways and sew the seams. Fold a chenille stick in half and place it inside the ear around the outside edge so you can bend it into position. Repeat for the second ear. Pin the ears in place using the picture as guidance, then sew them in place, pushing the two ends of the chenille stick inside the head to avoid any sharp ends protruding. Sew the head to the body.

Sew the side seam of the arm stuffing with toy filling as you go. Using MC, work three stitches over the paw to give the appearance of separate fingers. Repeat for the second arm. Sew it to the side seam of the dog, using the picture for guidance and placing the seam underneath the arm.

Sew the foot seam, stuffing with toy filling as you go. Sew the side seam of the leg and stuff with toy filling. Sew the stuffed foot to the end of the leg with the leg seam at the back. The cast-off end of the foot should be at the back. Sew the seam at the top of the leg together from side to side. Using MC work three stitches over the paw to give the appearance of separate toes. Repeat for the second foot and leg. Using the picture for guidance sew the legs to the body, making sure you sew them to a MC stripe. Sew the tail to the lowest CC stripe on the back of the body. The tail is not stuffed.

Pink Poodle

Glamorous Pink Poodle is a rosy delight! She is easy to make as her fluffy wristlets and anklets are knitted separately and sewn on after making up. Don't forget to give her some long eyelashes.

Materials
80m (87½yd) of pale pink 5-ply (sportweight) yarn
45m (49¼yd) of pale pink fluffy 10-ply (Aran) yarn
Small amount of black 4-ply (fingering) yarn
Two 6mm (¼in) black beads
Toy filling
Black sewing cotton and sewing needle
Small amount of narrow pink ribbon
Pink sewing cotton

Needles
3.25mm (UK 10, US 3) knitting needles
4.5mm (UK 7, US 7) knitting needles
2.75mm (UK 12, US 2) knitting needles

Tension
25 sts measured over 10cm (4in) and worked in SS with 3.25mm (UK 10, US 3) knitting needles and 5-ply (sportweight) yarn

Size
21cm (8¼in) from the bottom of the feet to top of the head

Body
Using pale pink fluffy 10-ply (Aran) yarn and 4.5mm (UK 7, US 7) knitting needles, cast on 12 sts and, starting with a knit row, work 4 rows in SS.
Next row: K2, (Kfb) twice, K4, (Kfb) twice, K2 [16 sts].
Work 3 rows in SS.
Next row: K3, (Kfb) twice, K6, (Kfb) twice, K3 [20 sts].
Work 3 rows in SS.
Next row: K4, (Kfb) twice, K8, (Kfb) twice, K4 [24 sts].
Purl 1 row.
Next row: K5, (Kfb) twice, K10, (Kfb) twice, K5. [28 sts].
Purl 1 row.
Next row: K6, (Kfb) twice, K12, (Kfb) twice, K6 [32 sts].
Work 7 rows in SS.
Next row: K6, (K2tog) twice, K12, (K2tog) twice, K6 [28 sts].
Purl 1 row.
Next row: K5, (K2tog) twice, K10, (K2tog) twice, K5 [24 sts].
Purl 1 row.
Next row: K4, (K2tog) twice, K8, (K2tog) twice, K4 [20 sts].
Next row: P3, (P2tog) twice, P6, (P2tog) twice, P3 [16 sts].
Cast off.

I'm feeling in the pink!

Legs (make two)

Using pale pink 5-ply (sportweight) yarn and 3.25mm (UK 10, US 3) knitting needles, cast on 14 sts. Starting with a knit row, work 14 rows in SS.

Cast off.

Feet (make two)

Using pale pink 5-ply (sportweight) yarn and 3.25mm (UK 10, US 3) knitting needles, cast on 7 sts and purl 1 row.

Next row: K1, M1, K to last st, M1, K1 [9 sts].

Next row: P1, M1, P to last st, M1, P1 [11 sts].

Work 6 rows in SS.

Next row: K1, ssK, K to last 3 sts, K2tog, K1 [9 sts].

Work 2 rows in SS.

Next row: P1, M1, P to last st, M1, P1 [11 sts].

Work 6 rows in SS.

Next row: K1, ssK, K to last 3 sts, K2tog, K1 [9 sts].

Next row: P1, P2tog, P to last 3 sts, P2togtbl, P1 [7 sts].

Knit 1 row.

Cast off.

Arms (make two)

Using pale pink 5-ply (sportweight) yarn and 3.25mm (UK 10, US 3) knitting needles, cast on 12 sts and, starting with a knit row, work 12 rows in SS.

Next row: K1, M1, K4, M1, K2, M1, K4, M1, K1 [16 sts].

Purl 1 row.

Next row: K1, M1, K6, M1, K2, M1, K6, M1, K1 [20 sts].

Work 3 rows in SS.

Next row: K1, ssK, K4, K2tog, K2, ssK, K4, K2tog, K1 [16 sts].

Purl 1 row.

Next row: K1, ssK, K2, K2tog, K2, ssK, K2, K2tog, K1 [12 sts].

Cast off using three needle cast off technique (see page 13).

Head

Using pale pink 5-ply (sportweight) yarn and 3.25mm (UK 10, US 3) knitting needles, cast on 10 sts.

Next row: K1, M1, K to last st, M1, K1 [12 sts].

Next row: P1, M1, P to last st, M1, P1 [14 sts].

Rep last two rows once more [18 sts].

Next row: K1, M1, K to last st, M1, K1 [20 sts].

Purl 1 row.

Rep last two rows once more [22 sts].

Next row: K10, M1, K2, M1, K10 [24 sts].

Next row: P11, M1, P2, M1, P11 [26 sts].

Next row: K12, M1, K2, M1, K12 [28 sts].

Next row: P13, M1, P2, M1, P13 [30 sts].

Next row: K14, M1, K2, M1, K14 [32 sts].

Next row: P15, M1, P2, M1, P15 [34 sts].

Work 6 rows in SS.

Next row: K1, ssK, K11, K2tog, K2, ssK, K11, K2tog, K1 [30 sts].

Purl 1 row.

Next row: K1, ssK, K9, K2tog, K2, ssK, K9, K2tog, K1 [26 sts].

Purl 1 row.

Next row: K1, ssK, K7, K2tog, K2, ssK, K7, K2tog, K1 [22 sts].

Next row: P1, P2tog, P5, P2togtbl, P2, P2tog, P5, P2togtbl, P1 [18 sts].

Cast off using three needle cast off technique (see page 13).

Nose

Using black 4-ply (fingering) yarn and 2.75mm (UK 12, US 2) knitting needles, cast on 3 sts.

Next row: (K1, M1) twice, K1 [5 sts].

Work 2 rows in SS.

Next row: P2tog, P1, P2tog [3 sts].

Next row: Sl1, K2tog, psso [1 st].

Thread yarn through rem st and fasten, leaving enough yarn to embroider the mouth.

Ears (make two)

Worked in GS.

Using pale pink fluffy 10-ply (Aran) yarn and 4.5mm (UK 7, US 7) knitting needles, cast on 5 sts and knit 6 rows.

Next row: K1, M1, K3, M1, K1 [7 sts].

Knit 5 rows.

Next row: K1, M1, K5, M1, K1 [9 sts].

Knit 5 rows.

Next row: K2tog, K to last 2 sts, K2tog [7 sts].

Rep last row once more [5 sts].

Cast off.

Tail

Using pale pink 5-ply (sportweight) yarn and 3.25mm (UK 10, US 3) knitting needles, cast on 8 sts and, starting with a knit row, work 6 rows in SS.

Next row: K2tog, K4, K2tog [6 sts].

Work 6 rows in SS.

Thread yarn through sts and fasten.

Fur cuffs (make two for arms and two for legs)

Using pale pink fluffy 10-ply (Aran) yarn and 4.5mm (UK 7, US 7) knitting needles, cast on 4 sts and, starting with a knit row, work in SS until long enough to go around arm/leg.

Cast off.

Pom-pom for tail

Worked in GS.

Using pale pink fluffy 10-ply (Aran) yarn and 4.5mm (UK 7, US 7) knitting needles, cast on 6 sts and knit 1 row.

Next row: Kfb, K to last st, Kfb [8 sts].

Knit 1 row.

Rep last two rows once more [10 sts].

Knit 5 rows.

Next row: K2tog, K to last 2 sts, K2tog [8 sts].

Knit 1 row.

Rep last two rows once more [6 sts].

Cast off.

Fluffy top of head

Worked in GS.

Using pale pink fluffy 10-ply (Aran) yarn and 4.5mm (UK 7, US 7) knitting needles, cast on 4 sts and knit 1 row.

Next row: K1, M1, K to last st, M1, K1 [6 sts].

Work 4 rows in GS.

Next row: K2tog, K to last 2 sts, K2tog [6 sts].

Cast off.

Making up

With the WS on the outside and the cast-off edge at the bottom, sew the body seam, stuffing with toy filling as you go. This seam will be at the back. Sew the bottom seam closed from side to side.

Placing the cast-off edge at the back of the head, sew the seam that will go underneath the head, stuffing with toy filling as you go. Sew the cast-on edges together up to the nose. To finish the head, see page 13 for instructions on how to gather the nose.

Pin the black beads in place as eyes using the picture as guidance. Sew in place. Run a thread from the back of one eye down to the base of the head and pull slightly to secure, then repeat for the second eye. This gives the eyes a much more realistic look. Embroider eyelashes using straight stitches and black sewing cotton.

Pin the fluffy top of the head in place, putting a tiny amount of toy filling inside. Sew in place. Pin the ears in place, using the picture as guidance, and then sew in place. Sew the black nose to the front of the head using 4-ply (fingering) yarn. Using the length of yarn left at the end of the nose, embroider the mouth using straight stitches. Pin the head to the body and sew it firmly in place.

Sew the foot seam, stuffing with toy filling as you go. Sew the side seam of one leg and stuff with toy filling. Sew the stuffed foot to the end of the leg with the leg seam at the back. The cast-off end of the foot should be towards the back. Sew the seam at the top of the leg together from side to side. Work three stitches over the paw to distinguish the separate toes. Repeat for the second leg and foot. Using the picture for guidance sew the legs to the body.

Fold one arm in half and sew the seam. The cast-off stitches of the arm form the paw. Stuff with toy filling and embroider claws on the paw, using pale pink yarn and straight stitches, and using the picture as guidance. Repeat for the second arm. The seam will be at the bottom of the arm. Pin the arms on to the side seams of the body and sew in place.

Using pale pink yarn, sew a cuff around each of the wrists and legs of the poodle, using the pictures for guidance. Sew the tail seam and sew to the back of the body, using the picture for guidance. The seam is placed underneath. The tail is not stuffed. Using pale pink fluffy yarn, stitch around the pom-pom and gather, stuffing with toy filling. Sew to the end of the tail. Make a bow using narrow ribbon and sew to the top of one ear using pink sewing thread and needle.

Outdoors Dog

Outdoors dog just wants to have fun and splash about in some puddles in his cute wellington boots. Do not forget to put his coat on if it is cold outside – it is easy to make with the row by row instructions.

Materials

45m (49¼yd) of oatmeal 10-ply (Aran) yarn
20m (22yd) of green 5-ply (sportweight) yarn
10m (11yd) of brown 5-ply (sportweight) yarn
35m (38¼yd) of cream 5-ply (sportweight) yarn
Small amount of black 4-ply (fingering) yarn
Toy filling
Two 6mm (¼in) black beads
Black sewing cotton and sewing needle
Two stitch markers
Chenille sticks
Stitch holder or spare needle

Needles

2.75mm (UK 12, US 2) knitting needles
3.25mm (UK 10, US 3) knitting needles
4mm (UK 8, US 6) knitting needles

Tension

9–10 sts measured over 5cm (2in) and worked in SS using 4mm (UK 8, US 6) knitting needles and 10-ply (Aran) yarn

Size

14cm (5½in) tall to the top of the head.

Body and front legs

Start at the bottom edge of the right foot.
Using oatmeal 10-ply (Aran) yarn and 4mm (UK 8, US 6) knitting needles, cast on 10 sts.
Next row: K2, (Kfb) three times, K5 [13 sts].
Purl 1 row.
Next row: K2, (K2tog) three times, K5 [10 sts].
Work 7 rows in SS.
Next row: Cast off 5 sts, K to end of row [5 sts].
Next row: Cast off 2 sts, P to end of row [3 sts].
Next row: K1, M1, K to end of row [4 sts].
Next row: Cast on 10 sts, P to last st, M1, P1 [15 sts].
Next row: K to last st M1, K1 [16 sts].
Work 19 rows in SS, placing a stitch marker at either end of row 10.
Next row: K to last 3 sts, K2tog, K1 [15 sts].
Next row: Cast off 10 sts, P to last 3 sts, P2togtbl, P1 [4 sts].
Next row: K1, K2tog, K1 [3 sts].
Next row: Cast on 2 sts, P to end of row [5 sts].
Next row: Cast on 5 sts, K to end of row [10 sts].
Work 7 rows in SS.
Next row: K2, (Kfb) three times, K5 [13 sts].
Purl 1 row.
Next row: K2, (K2tog) three times, K5 [10 sts].
Cast off (WS).

Belly

Using oatmeal 10-ply (Aran) yarn and 4mm (UK 8, US 6) knitting needles, cast on 4 sts. Starting with a knit row, work 4 rows in SS.
Next row: K1, M1, K2, M1, K1 [6 sts].
Work 5 rows in SS.
Next row: K1, M1, K4, M1, K1 [8 sts].
Work 21 rows in SS.

Next row: K1, ssK, K2, K2tog, K1 [6 sts].
Work 3 rows in SS.
Next row: K1, ssK, K2tog, K1 [4 sts].
Work 5 rows in SS.
Cast off.

Head

Start at the bottom of the head.
Using oatmeal 10-ply (Aran) yarn and 4mm (UK 8, US 6) knitting needles, cast on 10 sts and, starting with a knit row, work 2 rows in SS. Place these sts on a stitch holder or spare needle.

Using 10-ply (Aran) yarn and 4mm (UK 8, US 6) needles, cast on 10 sts and, starting with a knit row, work 2 rows in SS, making the second section.

Next row: With RS facing, K across 10 sts on needle and then K across 10 sts on holder [20 sts].
Purl 1 row.
Next row: K1, M1, K8, M1, K2, M1, K8, M1, K1 [24 sts].
Next row: P1, M1, P10, M1, P2, M1, P10, M1, P1 [28 sts].
Work 2 rows in SS.
Next row: K11, ssK, K2, K2tog, K11 [26 sts].
Next row: P10, P2tog, P2, P2togtbl, P10 [24 sts].
Next row: K9, ssK, K2, K2tog, K9 [22 sts].

Next row: P8, P2tog, P2, P2togtbl, P8 [20 sts].
Next row: K7, ssK, K2, K2tog, K7 [18 sts].
Purl 1 row.
Next row: K6, ssK, K2, K2tog, K6 [16 sts].
Next row: P1, P2tog, P2, P2tog, P2, P2togtbl, P2, P2togtbl, P1 [12 sts].
Cast off.

Back leg (right)

Using oatmeal 10-ply (Aran) yarn and 4mm (UK 8, US 6) knitting needles, cast on 10 sts.
Next row: K2, (Kfb) three times, K5 [13 sts].
Purl 1 row.
Next row: K2, (K2tog) three times, K5 [10 sts].
Work 3 rows in SS.
Next row: K8, w&t.
Next row: P3, w&t.
Next row: K to end of row.
Purl 1 row.
Next row: K1, M1, (K3, M1) twice, K3 [13 sts].
Purl 1 row.
Next row: Cast off 9 sts, M1, K3 [5 sts].
Next row: Cast off 2 sts, M1, P1, M1, P1 [5 sts].
* **Next row:** K1, M1, K to last st, M1, K1 [7 sts].
Next row: P1, M1, P to last st, M1, P1 [9 sts].
Work 4 rows in SS.
Next row: K1, ssK, K to last three sts, K2tog, K1 [7 sts].
Next row: P1, P2tog, P1, P2togtbl, P1 [5 sts].
Cast off.

I'm ready to go!

Back leg (left)
Using oatmeal 10-ply (Aran) yarn and 4mm (UK 8, US 6) knitting needles, cast on 10 sts.
Next row: K5, (Kfb) three times, K2 [13 sts].
Purl 1 row.
Next row: K5, (K2tog) three times, K2 [10 sts].
Work 3 rows in SS.
Next row: K5, w&t.
Next row: P3, w&t.
Next row: K to end of row.
Purl 1 row.

Next row: (K3, M1) three times, K1 [13 sts].
Purl 1 row.
Next row: Cast off 2 sts, M1, K to end of row [12 sts].
Next row: Cast off 9 sts, M1, P to last st, M1, P1 [5 sts].
Work as for back leg (right) from * to end.

Ears (make two)
Using oatmeal 10-ply (Aran) yarn and 4mm (UK 8, US 6) knitting needles, cast on 6 sts. Starting with a knit row, work 4 rows in SS.
Next row: K1, ssK, K2tog, K1 [4 sts].
Work 3 rows in SS.
Next row: K1, K2tog, K1 [3 sts].
Next row: Sl1, P2tog, psso [1 st].
Thread yarn through rem st to fasten, leaving a length of yarn for making up.

Tail
Using oatmeal 10-ply (Aran) yarn and 4mm (UK 8, US 6) knitting needles, cast on 4 sts. Work 4 rows in SS.
Next row: K1, M1, K to last st, M1, K1 [6 sts].
Purl 1 row.
Next row: K4, w&t.
Next row: P2, w&t.
Next row: K to end of row.
Work 3 rows in SS.
Cast off.

Nose
Using black 4-ply (fingering) yarn and 2.75mm (UK 12, US 2) knitting needles, cast on 3 sts.
Next row: (K1, M1) twice, K1 [5 sts].
Work 3 rows in SS.
Next row: ssK, K1, K2tog [3 sts].
Next row: Sl1, P2tog, psso [1 st].
Thread yarn through rem st to fasten, leaving a length of yarn long enough to embroider the mouth.

Making up

Starting with one of the front legs, thread a length of oatmeal 10-ply (Aran) yarn through the bottom edge of the foot and gather to form the bottom of the foot. Sew up the side seam and stuff firmly with toy filling, placing a chenille stick inside the toy filling. Repeat for the second front leg.

Matching the middle of the cast-off edge of the belly to the stitch marker at the back of the body, and the middle of the cast-on edge of the belly to the stitch marker at the front of the body, pin the belly in place. Stuff the body firmly with toy filling and sew the seams of the belly in place. Sew the cast-off edge of the top of each front leg to the belly, using the picture on the right for guidance.

Sew up both of the back legs in the same way as the front legs. Pin the top of the back leg to the body as shown in the picture, stuff gently with toy filling and sew in place, sewing the cast-off edge of the top of the leg to the belly.

Fold the cast-off edge of the head in half and sew the stitches together. Sew the head seam that will be at the bottom of the head, stuffing with toy filling. Taking the length of yarn from the last decreased stitch of the ear, use a darning needle to run the yarn down the edge stitches on one side of the ear and pull slightly to make the ear bend over. Repeat for the second ear but pull the yarn tighter to make the ear fold over more (see picture). Pin the ears in place using the picture for guidance, then sew them firmly in place. Using black sewing cotton, sew the two beads in place for eyes. Sew the black nose to the front of the head, placing the cast-on edge at the top, then use the length of yarn left at the end of the nose to embroider the mouth in place using straight stitches. Sew the head firmly to the front of the body.

Fold the tail in half and sew the seam. Sew it in place using the picture for guidance and placing the seam on the top.

Boots (make four)

Using brown 5-ply (sportweight) yarn and 3.25mm (UK 10, US 3) knitting needles, cast on 4 sts and knit 2 rows.

Next row: K1, M1, K2, M1, K1 [6 sts].

Knit 4 rows.

Next row: K1, (K2tog) twice, K1 [4 sts].

Knit 4 rows.

Cast on 8 sts at the beginning of the next two rows (knitting both rows) [20 sts].

Next row (RS): Change to green 5-ply (sportweight) yarn and, starting with a knit row, work 2 rows in SS.

Next row: K7, ssK, K2, K2tog, K7 [18 sts].

Next row: P6, P2tog, P2, P2togtbl, P6 [16 sts].

Next row: K5, ssK, K2, K2tog, K5 [14 sts].

Work 4 rows in SS.

Knit 2 rows.

Cast off loosely and evenly.

Making up

Sew up the back seam of the first boot. Sew the sole into place along the brown edge of the boot. Place a small amount of toy filling in the toe of the boot, then place the boot on the dog's leg. Repeat for the other three boots.

Coat

When working the cable section of the coat, please see the abbreviations on page 112.

Using cream 5-ply (sportweight) yarn and 3.25mm (UK 10, US 3) knitting needles, cast on 20 sts and work as follows:

Row 1: (P2, K4) three times, P2.

Row 2: (K2, P4) three times, K2.

Row 3: Cast on 6 sts at the beginning of the row, P2, K4, (P2, C4F) three times, P2 [26 sts].

Row 4: Cast on 6 sts at the beginning of the row, (K2, P4) five times, K2 [32 sts].

Row 5: (P2, K4) five times, P2.

Row 6: (K2, P4) five times, K2.

Row 7: (P2, C4F) five times, P2.

Row 8: As row 6.

Repeat rows 5–8 twice more.

Row 17: (P2, K4), twice, P1, cast off 6 sts, (K4, P2) twice (leaving you with two sets of 13 sts).

Row 18: Turn work and continue over first set of 13 sts. (K2, P4) twice, K1.

Row 19: Cast off 2 sts, K2, P2, C4f, P2 [11 sts].

Row 20: K2, P4, K2, P3.

Row 21: Cast off 1 st, K1, P2, K4, P2 [10 sts].

Row 22: K2, P4, K2, P2.

Row 23: K2, P2, C4F, P2.

Row 24: As row 22.

Row 25: K2, P2, K4, P2.

Row 26: As row 22.

Row 27: As row 23.

Row 28: As row 22.

Repeat rows 25–28 once more.

Cast off.

With WS facing, rejoin yarn to rem 13 sts.

Row 18: K1, P4, K2, P4, K2.

Row 19: P2, C4F, P2, K4, P1.

Row 20: Cast off 2 sts, P2, K2, P4, K2 [11 sts].

Row 21: P2, K4, P2, K3.

Row 22: Cast off 1 st, P1, K2, P4, K2 [10 sts].

Row 23: P2, C4F, P2, K2.

Row 24: P2, K2, P4, K2.

Row 25: P2, K4, P2, K2.

Row 26: As row 24.

Row 27: As row 23.

Row 28: As row 24.

Repeat rows 25–28 once more.

Cast off.

Making up

With RS facing, pick up and knit 72 sts around the outside edge of the coat. Work 4 rows in K2, P2, rib. Cast off.

With RS facing pick up and knit 32 sts around the neck edge of the coat. Work 8 rows in K2, P2 rib. Cast off.

Sew the front seam of the coat together, from the top of the neck rib to the bottom of the edging rib. Place the coat on the dog and fold the collar over.

Christmas Dog

Get into the Christmas spirit with Christmas Dog and his fun sweater, which is knitted using the Fair Isle technique (see page 12), and finished off with a little embroidery. His antlers really help to get him into the party spirit!

Materials
100m (109⅜yd) of brown 10-ply (Aran) yarn
Small amount of black 4-ply (fingering) yarn
Toy filling
Two 8mm (⅜in) black shanked buttons

Needles
4mm (UK 8, US 6) knitting needles
2.75mm (UK 12, US 2) knitting needles

Tension
9–10 sts measured over 5cm (2in) and worked in SS using 4mm (UK 8, US 6) knitting needles and 10-ply (Aran) yarn

Size
26cm (10¼in) from top of the head to the bottom of the feet

Body (front)
Using brown 10-ply (Aran) yarn and 4mm (UK 8, US 6) knitting needles, cast on 12 sts and, starting with a knit row, work 2 rows in SS.
Next row: K1, M1, K to last st, M1, K1 [14 sts].
Work 3 rows in SS.
Next row: K1, M1, K5, M1, K2, M1, K5, M1, K1 [18 sts].
Work 3 rows in SS.
Next row: K1, M1, K7, M1, K2, M1, K7, M1, K1 [22 sts].
Work 3 rows in SS.
Next row: K1, M1, K9, M1, K2, M1, K9, M1, K1 [26 sts].
Purl 1 row.
Next row: K1, M1, K11, M1, K2, M1, K11, M1, K1 [30 sts].

Work 13 rows in SS.
Next row: K1, ssK, K9, K2tog, K2, ssK, K9, K2tog, K1 [26 sts].
Purl 1 row.
Next row: K1, ssK, K7, K2tog, K2, ssK, K7, K2tog, K1 [22 sts].
Purl 1 row.
Next row: K1, ssK, K5, K2tog, K2, ssK, K5, K2tog, K1 [18 sts].
Next row: P1, P2tog, P3, P2togtbl, P2, P2tog, P3, P2togtbl, P1 [14 sts].
Next row: K1, ssK, K1, K2tog, K2, ssK, K1, K2tog, K1 [10 sts].
Next row: P1, (P2tog, P2togtbl) twice, P1 [6 sts].
Cast off.

Body (back)
Using brown 10-ply (Aran) yarn and 4mm (UK 8, US 6) knitting needles, cast on 10 sts and, starting with a knit row, work 2 rows in SS.
Next row: K1, M1, K to last st, M1, K1 [12 sts].
Work 3 rows in SS.
Rep last four rows once more [14 sts].
Next row: K1, M1, K5, M1, K2, M1, K5, M1, K1 [18 sts].
Work 3 rows in SS.
Next row: K1, M1, K7, M1, K2, M1, K7, M1, K1 [22 sts].
Work 3 rows in SS.
Next row: K1, M1, K9, M1, K2, M1, K9, M1, K1 [26 sts].
Work 7 rows in SS.
Next row: K1, ssK, K7, K2tog, K2, ssK, K7, K2tog, K1 [22 sts].
Purl 1 row.
Next row: K1, ssK, K5, K2tog, K2, ssK, K5, K2tog, K1 [18 sts].
Purl 1 row.

Next row: K1, ssK, K3, K2tog, K2, ssK, K3, K2tog, K1 [14 sts].

Purl 1 row.

Next row: K1, ssK, K1, K2tog, K2, ssK, K1, K2tog, K1 [10 sts].

Next row: P1, (P2tog, P2togtbl) twice, P1 [6 sts].

Cast off.

Legs (make two)

Using brown 10-ply (Aran) yarn and 4mm (UK 8, US 6) knitting needles, cast on 14 sts and, starting with a knit row, work 12 rows in SS.

Next row: K6, M1, K2, M1, K6 [16 sts].

Next row: P7, M1, P2, M1, P7 [18 sts].

Next row: K8, M1, K2, M1, K8 [20 sts].

Next row: P9, M1, P2, M1, P9 [22 sts].

Next row: K10, M1, K2, M1, K10 [24 sts].

Next row: P11, M1, P2, M1, P11 [26 sts].

Work 4 rows in SS.

Next row: K1, ssK, K7, K2tog, K2, ssK, K7, K2tog, K1 [22 sts].

Cast off rem 22 sts using the three needle cast off technique (see page 13).

Arms (make two)

Using brown 10-ply (Aran) yarn and 4mm (UK 8, US 6) knitting needles, cast on 12 sts and, starting with a knit row, work 12 rows in SS.

Next row: K1, M1, K4, M1, K2, M1, K4, M1, K1 [16 sts].

Purl 1 row.

Next row: K1, M1, K6, M1, K2, M1, K6, M1, K1 [20 sts].

Work 3 rows in SS.

Next row: K1, ssK, K4, K2tog, K2, ssK, K4, K2tog, K1 [16 sts].

Purl 1 row.

Cast off using the three needle cast-off technique (see page 13).

Head

Using brown 10-ply (Aran) yarn and 4mm (UK 8, US 6) knitting needles, cast on 14 sts and purl 1 row.

Next row: K1, M1, K to last st, M1, K1 [16 sts].

Next row: P1, M1, P to last st, M1, P1 [18 sts].

Rep last two rows once more [22 sts].

Next row: K1, M1, K to last st, M1, K1 [24 sts].

Purl 1 row.

Rep last two rows once more [26 sts].

Next row: K12, M1, K2, M1, K12 [28 sts].

Next row: P13, M1, P2, M1, P13 [30 sts].

Next row: K14, M1, K2, M1, K14 [32 sts].

Next row: P15, M1, P2, M1, P15 [34 sts].

Next row: K16, M1, K2, M1, K16 [36 sts].

Next row: P17, M1, P2, M1, P17 [38 sts].

Work 8 rows in SS.

Next row: K1, ssK, K13, K2tog, K2, ssK, K13, K2tog, K1 [34 sts].

Purl 1 row.

Next row: K1, ssK, K11, K2tog, K2, ssK, K11, K2tog, K1 [30 sts].

Purl 1 row.

Next row: K1, ssK, K9, K2tog, K2, ssK, K9, K2tog, K1 [26 sts].

Next row: P1, P2tog, P7, P2togtbl, P2, P2tog, P7, P2togtbl, P1 [22 sts].

Next row: K1, ssK, K5, K2tog, K2, ssK, K5, K2tog, K1 [18 sts].

Cast off rem 18 sts using three needle cast off technique (see page 13).

Ears (make two)

Using brown 10-ply (Aran) yarn and 4mm (UK 8, US 6) knitting needles, cast on 7 sts and, starting with a knit row, work 6 rows in SS.

Next row: ssK, K to last 2 sts, K2tog [5 sts].

Purl 1 row.

Rep last two rows once more [3 sts].

Next row: Sl1, K2tog, psso [1 st].

Next row: Kfbf [3 sts].

Purl 1 row.

Next row: K1, M1, K to last st, M1, K1 [5 sts].

Purl 1 row.

Rep last two rows once more [7 sts].

Work 6 rows in SS.

Cast off.

Nose

Using black 4-ply (fingering) yarn and 2.75mm (UK 12, US 2) knitting needles, cast on 7 sts and, starting with a knit row, work 2 rows in SS.

Next row: K1, ssK, K1, K2tog, K1 [5 sts].

Purl 1 row.

Next row: ssK, K1, K2tog [3 sts].

Next row: Sl1, P2tog, psso [1 st].

Fasten off rem st, leaving a length of yarn long enough to embroider the mouth.

Tail

Using brown 10-ply (Aran) yarn and 4mm (UK 8, US 6) knitting needles, cast on 8 sts and, starting with a knit row, work 2 rows in SS.

* Next row: K6, w&t.

Next row: P4, w&t.

Next row: K to end of row.

Purl 1 row. *

Rep from * to * once more.

Next row: ssK, K to last 2 sts, K2tog [6 sts].

Purl 1 row.

Rep last two rows once more [4 sts].

Thread yarn through rem sts and fasten.

Making up

Pin the side seams of the body pieces together with the cast-off edge at the bottom. Stuff with toy filling and sew up the seams.

To make up the head, place the cast-off edge at the back of the head, sew up the seam that will go underneath the head, stuffing with toy filling as you go. Sew the cast-on edges together up to the nose. To finish the head see page 13 for instructions on how to gather the nose.

Sew the black-shanked buttons in place as eyes, using the picture as guidance. Run a thread from the back of one eye down to the base of the head and pull slightly to secure. Repeat for the second eye. This gives the eyes a much more realistic look.

With WS together, fold one ear in half and carefully sew the side seams. Repeat for the second ear. Pin the ears in place on the top of the head, then sew both in place, curving them slightly and using the picture for guidance.

Sew the nose to the front of the face and embroider the mouth using the length of yarn left at the end of the nose and straight stitches.

Sew the head to the body matching the seam under the head with the centre of the body.

Fold one arm in half and sew the seam. Stuff with toy filling, then embroider claws on the paw using brown 10-ply (Aran) yarn and straight stitches, using the picture as guidance. Repeat for the second arm. Pin the arms on to the side seams of the body and sew, placing the seam underneath the arm.

Sew the back seam of one leg, stuffing with toy filling. Repeat for the second leg and pin both legs in place on to the bottom seam of the body. Use the picture for guidance when placing the legs.

Sew the seam of the tail (this will be at the top when it is sewn on to the body) and place a small amount of toy filling inside. Sew in place at the bottom of the body.

Antlers

Materials

- Small amount of dark brown 4-ply (fingering) yarn (used double)
- Small amount of red 4-ply (fingering) yarn
- Chenille stick

Needles

- 4mm (UK 8, US 6) knitting needles
- 2.75mm (UK 12, US 2) knitting needles

Long antler pieces (make two)

Using a double strand of dark brown 4-ply (fingering) yarn and 4mm (UK 8, US 6) knitting needles, cast on 6 sts and work in SS until work measures 6cm (2⅜in). Cast off.

Short antler pieces (make four)

Using a double strand of dark brown yarn and 4mm (UK 8, US 6) knitting needles, cast on 6 sts and work in SS until work measures 2cm (⅞in). Cast off.

Headband

Using red 4-ply (fingering) yarn and 2.75mm (UK 12, US 2) knitting needles, cast on 10 sts and work in SS until work measures 10cm (4in). Cast off.

Making up

To make one antler, sew the side seam of a long piece, sewing a stitch in from the edge and using mattress stitch (see page 12) to make the antler stand up better. Sew two small pieces in the same way and sew one to each side of the long piece using the picture as guidance. Repeat for the second antler.

Fold the headband and sew the side seam, inserting a double length of chenille stick as you go. Finish sewing the seam. Sew each antler on to the headband placing them in the centre approximately 1cm (½in) apart, using the picture for guidance.

Bend the headband slightly, so that it fits comfortably on the dog's head.

Christmas sweater

Materials

- 80m (87½yd) of royal blue 4-ply (fingering) yarn
- 10m (11yd) of brown 4-ply (fingering) yarn
- 3m (3¼yd) of dark brown 4-ply (fingering) yarn
- Small amount of red 4-ply (fingering) yarn
- Sparkly white 4-ply (fingering) yarn

Needles

- 3mm (UK 11, US 2/3) knitting needles

Tension

Approximately 7 sts to 2.5cm (1in), measured over SS using 3mm (UK 11, US 2/3) needles

Front

Using royal blue 4-ply (fingering) yarn and 3mm (UK 11, US 2/3) knitting needles, cast on 40 sts and work 4 rows in K2, P2 rib.

Starting with a knit row, continue in SS following the reindeer chart (top left on opposite page), using the Fair Isle technique (see page 13).

Continue following the chart and work the armholes as follows:

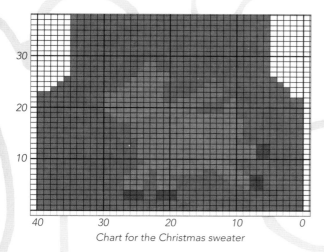

30

20

10

40   30   20   10   0

Chart for the Christmas sweater

Cast off 2 sts at the beginning of the next two rows.
[36 sts].
Row 1: K1, ssK, K to last 3 sts, K2tog, K1 [34 sts].
Row 2: P1, P2tog, P to last 3 sts, P2togtbl, P1
[32 sts].
Rep row 1 once more [30 sts]. *
Work 11 rows in SS.
Shape neckline as follows:
Next row: K11, cast off 8 sts, K10.
Working over the first set of 11 sts, P 1 row.
Next row: Cast off 2 sts at the beginning of the row
[9 sts].
Purl 1 row.
Rep last two rows once more [7 sts].
Next row: K1, ssK, K4 [6 sts].
Purl 1 row.
Cast off.
With WS facing rejoin yarn to rem 11 sts.
Cast off 2 sts at the beginning of the row [9 sts].
Knit 1 row.
Rep last two rows once more [7 sts].
Purl 1 row.
Next row: K4, K2tog, K1 [6 sts].
Purl 1 row.
Cast off.

Back

Using royal blue 4-ply (fingering) yarn and 3mm
(UK 11, US 2/3) knitting needles, cast on 40 sts
and work as for front to the end of the armhole
shaping (marked with *).
Starting with a purl row, work 15 rows in SS.

Next row: K10, cast off 10 sts, K9.
Working over the first set of 10 sts, purl 1 row.
Next row: Cast off 4 sts, K5 [6 sts].
Purl 1 row.
Cast off. With WS facing, rejoin yarn to rem 10 sts.
Cast off 4 sts, P5 [6 sts].
Work 2 rows in SS.
Cast off.

Sleeves (make two)

Using royal blue 4-ply (fingering) yarn and 3mm (UK
11, US 2/3) knitting needles, cast on 28 sts and work
4 rows in K2, P2 rib.
Starting with a knit row, work 2 rows in SS.
Next row: K1, M1, K to last st, M1, K1 [30 sts].
Work 3 rows in SS.
Rep last four rows once more [32 sts].
Work 2 rows in SS.
Cast off 2 sts at the beginning of the next two rows
[28 sts].
Next row: K1, ssK, K to last 3 sts, K2tog, K1 [26 sts].
Purl 1 row.
Rep last two rows once more [24 sts].
Cast off.

Making up

Join right shoulder seam. Using royal blue 4-ply
(fingering) yarn and with RS facing, pick up and knit
24 sts around the front neckline and 20 sts around the
back neck shaping [44 sts].

Work 4 rows in K2, P2 rib and cast off in rib. Join
the left shoulder seam. Sew the sleeves in place and
sew the side seams and underarm seams.

Embroider details on to the reindeer, using the
picture below for guidance.

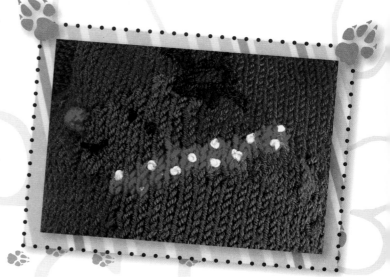

Danger Dog

Look! Up in the sky! Danger Dog is here! This tiny superhero is ready for action in his hat, cape and legwarmers. The lightning strike on his cape is knitted using the Fair Isle technique (see page 12).

Materials
57m (62⅜yd) of grey 5-ply (sportweight) yarn
Small amount of black 4-ply (fingering) yarn
Two 6mm (¼in) black beads
Toy filling
Black sewing cotton and sewing needle
Chenille sticks
Stitch markers

Needles
3.25mm (UK 10, US 3) knitting needles
2.75mm (UK 12, US 2) knitting needles

Tension
25 sts measured over 10cm (4in) and worked in SS using 3.25mm (UK 10, US 3) knitting needles and 5-ply (sportweight) yarn

Size
14cm (5¾in) from nose to tail

Body and front legs
Start at the bottom edge of right foot.
Using grey 5-ply (sportweight) yarn and 3.25mm (UK 10, US 3) knitting needles, cast on 10 sts.
* Next row: K5, turn.
Next row: P3, turn.
Next row: K3, turn.
Next row: P3, turn.
Next row: Knit to end of row.
Next row: P5, P3B, P2. *

Work 12 rows in SS.
Next row: Cast off 5 sts, K to end of row [5 sts].
Next row: Cast off 2 sts, P to end of row [3 sts].
Next row: K1, M1, K to end of row [4 sts].
Next row: Cast on 14 sts, P to last st, M1, P1 [19 sts].
Knit 1 row.
Next row: Cast on 2 sts and P to end of row [21 sts].
Work 27 rows in SS, placing a stitch marker at either end of row 13.
Next row: Cast off 2 sts, P to end of row [19 sts].
Knit 1 row.
Next row: Cast off 14 sts, P to last 3 sts, P2togtbl, P1 [4 sts].
Next row: K1, K2tog, K1 [3 sts].
Next row: Cast on 2 sts, P to end of row [5 sts].
Next row: Cast on 5 sts, K to end of row [10 sts].
Work 13 rows in SS.
Work from * to *.
Cast off.

Belly
Using grey 5-ply (sportweight) yarn and 3.25mm (UK 10, US 3) knitting needles, cast on 5 sts. Starting with a knit row, work 4 rows in SS.
Next row: K1, M1, K3, M1, K1 [7 sts].
Work 5 rows in SS.
Next row: K1, M1, K5, M1, K1 [9 sts].
Work 15 rows in SS.
Next row: K1, ssK, K3, K2tog, K1 [7 sts].
Work 17 rows in SS.
Next row: K1, ssK, K1, K2tog, K1 [5 sts].
Work 5 rows in SS.
Cast off.

Back leg (right)

Using grey 5-ply (sportweight) yarn and 3.25mm (UK 10, US 3) knitting needles, cast on 10 sts.

Next row: K5, turn.
Next row: P3, turn.
Next row: K3, turn.
Next row: P3, turn.
Next row: K to end of row.
Next row: P5, P3B, P2.
Work 12 rows in SS.
Next row: Cast off 5 sts, K to end of row [5 sts].
Next row: Cast off 1 st, P to end of row [4 sts].
* **Next row:** K1, M1, K to last st, M1, K1 [6 sts].
Next row: P1, M1, P to last st, M1, P1 [8 sts].
Rep last two rows once more [12 sts].
Work 6 rows in SS.
Next row: K1, ssK, K to last three sts, K2tog, K1 [10 sts].
Next row: P1, P2tog, P to last 3 sts, P2togtbl, P1 [8 sts].
Next row: K1, ssK, K to last three sts, K2tog, K1 [6 sts].
Cast off. *

Back leg (left)

Using grey 5-ply (sportweight) yarn and 3.25mm (UK 10, US 3) knitting needles, cast on 10 sts.
Next row: K8, turn.
Next row: P3, turn.
Next row: K3, turn.
Next row: P3, turn.
Next row: K to end of row.
Next row: P2, P3B, P5.
Work 12 rows in SS.
Next row: Cast off 1 st, K to end of row [9 sts].
Next row: Cast off 5 sts, P to end of row [4 sts].
Work as for back leg (right) from * to *.

Head

Using grey 5-ply (sportweight) yarn, cast on 10 sts.
Next row: K1, M1, K to last st, M1, K1 [12 sts].
Next row: P1, M1, P to last st, M1, P1 [14 sts].
Rep last two rows once more [18 sts].
Next row: K1, M1, K to last st, M1, K1 [20 sts].
Purl 1 row.

Rep last two rows once more [22 sts].
Next row: K10, M1, K2, M1, K10 [24 sts].
Next row: P11, M1, P2, M1, P11 [26 sts].
Next row: K12, M1, K2, M1, K12 [28 sts].
Next row: P13, M1, P2, M1, P13 [30 sts].
Next row: K14, M1, K2, M1, K14 [32 sts].
Next row: P15, M1, P2, M1, P15 [34 sts].
Work 6 rows in SS.
Next row: K1, ssK, K11, K2tog, K2, ssK, K11, K2tog, K1 [30 sts].
Purl 1 row.
Next row: K1, ssK, K9, K2tog, K2, ssK, K9, K2tog, K1 [26 sts].
Purl 1 row.
Next row: K1, ssK, K7, K2tog, K2, ssK, K7, K2tog, K1 [22 sts].
Next row: P1, P2tog, P5, P2togtbl, P2, P2tog, P5, P2togtbl, P1 [18 sts].
Cast off using the three needle cast off technique (see page 13).

Nose

Using black 4-ply (fingering) yarn and 2.75mm (UK 12, US 2) knitting needles, cast on 3 sts.
Next row: (K1, M1) twice, K1 [5 sts].
Work 2 rows in SS.
Next row: P2tog, P1, P2tog [3 sts].
Next row: Sl1, K2tog, psso [1 st].
Thread yarn through rem st and fasten, leaving a length of yarn long enough to embroider the mouth.

Ears (make four)

Using grey 5-ply (sportweight) yarn and 3.25mm (UK 10, US 3) knitting needles, cast on 6 sts and, starting with a knit row, work 4 rows in SS.
Next row: K2tog, K2, K2tog [4 sts].
Purl 1 row.
Next row: K2tog twice [2 sts].
Next row: P2tog [1 st].
Thread yarn through rem st and fasten.

Tail

Using grey 5-ply (sportweight) yarn and 3.25mm (UK 10, US 3) knitting needles cast on 7 sts and, starting with a knit row, work 6 rows in SS.
Next row: K1, K2tog, K1, K2tog, K1 [5 sts].
Work 7 rows in SS.
Thread yarn through sts and fasten.

Making up

Starting with one of the front legs, thread a length of yarn through the bottom edge of the foot and gather to form the bottom of the foot. Sew the side seam and stuff with toy filling, placing a chenille stick inside the toy filling. Repeat for the second front leg.

Matching the middle of the cast-off edge of the belly to the stitch marker at the back of the body and the middle of the cast-on edge of the belly to the stitch marker at the front of the body, pin the belly in place. Stuff the body firmly with toy filling, sewing the side seams of the belly in place. Sew the cast-off edge of the top of each front leg to the belly, pushing the end of the chenille stick inside the body.

Sew each back leg in the same way as the front legs. Pin the top of the back leg to the body as shown in the picture, stuff gently with toy filling and sew in place, sewing the cast-off edge of the top of the leg to the belly.

To make up the head, place the cast-off edge at the back of the head, sew the seam that will go underneath the head, stuffing with toy filling as you go. Sew the cast-on edges together up to the nose.

To finish the head, gather the nose using the instructions on page 13.

Sew the black beads in place as eyes, using the picture as guidance. Run a thread from the back of one eye down to the base of the head and pull slightly, secure. Repeat for the second eye. This gives the eyes a much more realistic look.

With WS together, sew two ear pieces together. Repeat for the second ear. Pin the ears in place, leaving a 2cm (¾in) gap between them and using the picture as guidance. Sew them in place.

Sew the black nose to the front of the head using 4-ply (fingering) yarn and embroider the mouth using the length of yarn left at the end of the nose and straight stitches.

Pin the head to the body, using the picture as guidance and sew firmly in place. Sew the tail seam and insert a chenille stick. Place a small amount of toy filling in the base of the tail. Poke the end of the chenille stick into the body to secure it and sew the tail in place.

Danger Dog outfit

Materials

35m (38¼yd) of blue 5-ply (sportweight) yarn
15m (16½yd) of lime 5-ply (sportweight) yarn
Small star button

Needles

3.25mm (UK 10, US 3) knitting needles

Cape

Using blue 5-ply (sportweight) yarn and 3.25mm (UK 10, US 3) knitting needles, cast on 28 sts and work 4 rows in GS.

Continue working as follows and at the same time work the lightning flash chart over the centre 8 sts and the next 20 rows.

Next row: Knit all sts.
Next row: K3, P to last 3 sts, K3.
Next row: K2, ssK, K to last 4 sts, K2tog, K2 [26 sts].
Next row: K3, P to last 3 sts, K3.
Rep last two rows a further six times [14 sts].
Next row: K2, ssK, K to last 4 sts, K2tog, K2 [12 sts].
Next row: K3, P to last 3 sts, K3.
Next row: Cast on 6 sts, K9, ssK, K2, K2tog, K3 [16 sts].

Next row: Cast on 6 sts, K to end of row [22 sts].
Next row: K to last 4 sts, K2tog, yo, K2 [this forms a buttonhole].
Knit 1 row.
Cast off.

Leggings (make four)

Using blue 5-ply (sportweight) yarn and 3.25mm (UK 10, US 3) knitting needles, cast on 12 sts and knit 1 row.
Starting with a knit row, work 8 rows in SS.
Purl 1 row.
Cast off.

Lightning points (make four)

Using lime 5-ply (sportweight) yarn and 3.25mm (UK 10, US 3) knitting needles, cast on 4 sts.
* Work 2 rows in GS.
Next row: K2tog, K2 [3 sts].
Next row: K1, K2tog [2 sts].
Next row: K2tog [1 st].
Next row: K1. *
Cast on 3 sts at the beginning of the next row, K to end of row [4 sts].
Rep from * to * once more.
Cast off rem 1 st.

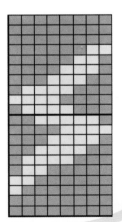

Chart for Danger
Dog's cape

82

Hat (make two)

Using blue 5-ply (sportweight) yarn and 3.25mm (UK 10, US 3) knitting needles, cast on 22 sts and, starting with a knit row, work 2 rows in SS.

Next row: K17, w&t.

Next row: P4, P2tog, P2togtbl, P4, w&t.

Next row: K3, ssK, K2tog, K2, w&t.

Next row: P1, P2tog, P2togtbl, P1, w&t.

Knit to end of row.

Knit 1 row.

Change to lime 5-ply (sportweight) yarn.

Cast off loosely and evenly.

Sew the cast-on edges of the two hat pieces together, leaving two holes for ears to go through, 2cm (¾in) apart.

Using lime 5-ply (sportweight) yarn and 3.25mm (UK 10, US 3) knitting needles and with right side facing, pick up and K 8 sts along one side edge to make a chin strap.

Starting with a WS row, purl 1 row.

Next row: K1, ssK, K to last 3 sts, K2tog, K1 [6 sts].

Purl 1 row.

Rep last two rows once more [4 sts].

Work six rows in SS.

Thread yarn though sts and fasten.

Rep these instructions to make a chin strap on the other side of the hat.

Spikes (make three)

Using lime 5-ply (sportweight) yarn and 3.25mm (UK 10, US 3) knitting needles, cast on 5 sts and knit 2 rows.

Next row: K2tog, K to end of row [4 sts].

Next row: K to last 2 sts, K2tog [3 sts].

Rep last two rows once more [1 st].

Thread yarn through rem st and fasten.

Making up

Sew all the ends in and lightly press the cape. Sew the star button on to the cape neckband on the opposite side to the buttonhole.

Sew the spikes to the centre top of the hat, using the picture for guidance. Sew the two chinstrap ends together and place the hat on the head, pulling the ears through the holes.

Sew the side seam of the leggings; this seam will be at the back. Sew the three lightning points along the back seam of the leggings, using the picture for guidance. Slide each legging on to Danger Dog's legs.

Best in Show

This scruffy little pup has won the judges' hearts with his appealing expression and scooped the Best in Show prize and a giant bone! Scruffy pup is knitted in a textured yarn which makes him very cuddly.

Materials
80m (87½yd) of fluffy light brown 10-ply (Aran) yarn
Small amount of red and black 4-ply (fingering) yarn
Toy filling
Two 10mm (⅜in) black shanked buttons
Black sewing cotton and sewing needle
Small piece of cardboard

Needles
4.5mm (UK 7, US 7) knitting needles
2.75mm (UK 12, US 2) knitting needles

Tension
15 sts measured over 10cm (4in) and worked in SS using 4.5mm (UK 7, US 7) knitting needles and 10-ply (Aran) yarn

Size
21cm (8¼in) high when sitting (see opposite)

Note
All pieces of the dog, except for the ears, are knitted in SS. When sewing together, the WS is on the outside as this side is more fluffy.

Body and base
Using light brown 10-ply (Aran) yarn and 4.5mm (UK 7, US 7) knitting needles, cast on 20 sts and, starting with a knit row, work 2 rows in SS.
Next row: K1, M1, K8, M1, K2, M1, K8, M1, K1 [24 sts].
Purl 1 row.
Next row: K11, (Kfb) twice, K11 [26 sts].
Purl 1 row.
Next row: K12, (Kfb) twice, K12 [28 sts].
Purl 1 row.
Next row: K13, (Kfb) twice, K13 [30 sts].

Purl 1 row.
Next row: K14, (Kfb) twice, K14 [32 sts].
Purl 1 row.
Next row: K15, (Kfb) twice, K15 [34 sts].
Purl 1 row.
Next row: K16, (Kfb) twice, K16 [36 sts].
Work 9 rows in SS.
Cast off 14 sts at the beginning of the next two rows [8 sts].
Work 2 rows in SS.
Next row: K1, M1, K to last st, M1, K1 [10 sts].
Work 7 rows in SS.
Next row: K1, K2tog, K to last 3 sts, K2tog, K1 [8 sts].
Purl 1 row.
Rep last two rows once more [6 sts].
Cast off.

Front legs (make two)
Using light brown 10-ply (Aran) yarn and 4.5mm (UK 7, US 7) knitting needles, cast on 9 sts.
Next row: K6, turn.
Next row: P3, turn.
Next row: K3, turn.
Next row: P3, turn.
Next row: K to end of row.
Purl 1 row.
Work 14 rows in SS.
Cast off 1 st at the beg of the next two rows [7 sts].
Cast off 2 sts at the beg of the next two rows [3 sts].
Cast off.

Back legs (make two)
Using light brown 10-ply (Aran) yarn and 4.5mm (UK 7, US 7) knitting needles cast on 9 sts.
Next row: K6, turn.
Next row: P3, turn.
Next row: K3, turn.
Next row: P3, turn.

Next row: K to end of row.
Purl 1 row.
Work 8 rows in SS.
Cast off.

Head

Using light brown 10-ply (Aran) yarn and 4.5mm (UK 7, US 7) knitting needles, cast on 10 sts and purl 1 row.

Next row: K1, M1, K to last st, M1, K1 [12 sts].
Next row: P1, M1, P to last st, M1, P1 [14 sts].
Rep last two rows once more [18 sts].
Work 2 rows in SS.
Next row: K8, M1, K2, M1, K8 [20 sts].
Next row: P9, M1, P2, M1, P9 [22 sts].
Next row: K10, M1, K2, M1, K10 [24 sts].
Next row: P11, M1, P2, M1, P11 [26 sts].
Next row: K12, M1, K2, M1, K12 [28 sts].
Next row: P13, M1, P2, M1, P13 [30 sts].
Work 6 rows in SS.
Next row: K1, ssK, K9, K2tog, K2, ssK, K9, K2tog, K1 [26 sts].
Purl 1 row.
Next row: K1, ssK, K7, K2tog, K2, ssK, K7, K2tog, K1 [22 sts].
Next row: P1, P2tog, P5, P2togtbl, P2, P2tog, P5, P2togtbl, P1 [18 sts].
Next row: K1, ssK, K3, K2tog, K2, ssK, K3, K2tog, K1 [14 sts].
Cast off using the three needle cast off technique (see page 13).

Ears (make two)

Using light brown 10-ply (Aran) yarn and 4.5mm (UK 7, US 7) knitting needles, cast on 7 sts and work 8 rows in GS.
Next row: K1, ssK, K1, K2tog, K1 [5 sts].
Knit 1 row.
Next row: ssK, K1, K2tog [3 sts].
Next row: Sl1, K2tog, psso [1 st].
Fasten off rem st.

Nose

Using black 4-ply (fingering) yarn and 2.75mm (UK 12, US 2) knitting needles, cast on 6 sts and, starting with a knit row, work 4 rows in SS.
Next row: K2tog, K2, K2tog [4 sts].
Next row: (P2tog) twice [2 sts].
Next row: K2tog.
Thread yarn through rem st and fasten, leaving a length of yarn long enough to embroider the mouth.

Tail

Using light brown 10-ply (Aran) yarn and 4.5mm (UK 7, US 7) knitting needles, cast on 8 sts and, starting with a knit row, work 6 rows in SS.
* Next row: K5, w&t.
Next row: P3, w&t.
Next row: K to end of row.
Purl 1 row. *
Rep from * to * once more.
Next row: K1, K2tog, K2, K2tog, K1 [6 sts].
Thread yarn through rem sts and fasten.

Rosette

Centre

Using red 4-ply (fingering) yarn and 2.75mm (UK 12, US 2) knitting needles, cast on 5 sts.
* Purl 1 row.
Next row: K1, M1, K to last st, M1, K1 [7 sts].
Purl 1 row.
Rep last two rows once more [9 sts].
Work 4 rows in SS.
Next row: K1, ssK, K to last 3 sts, K2tog, K1 [7 sts].
Purl 1 row.
Rep last two rows once more [5 sts]. *
Purl 1 row. (On the RS, this creates a fold line).
Rep from * to * once more and then cast off rem 5 sts.

Frill

Using red 4-ply (fingering) yarn and 2.75mm (UK 12, US 2) knitting needles, cast on 7 sts.
Work the following 20 row pattern and rep 5 more times, then cast off.

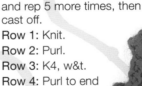
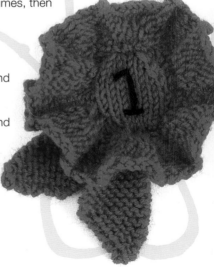

Row 1: Knit.
Row 2: Purl.
Row 3: K4, w&t.
Row 4: Purl to end of row.
Row 5: K5, w&t.
Row 6: Purl to end of row.
Row 7: K4, w&t.
Row 8: Purl to end of row.
Row 9: Knit.
Row 10: Purl.
Row 11: Purl.
Row 12: Knit.

Row 13: P4, w&t.
Row 14: Knit to end of row.
Row 15: P5, w&t.
Row 16: Knit to end of row.
Row 17: P4, w&t.
Row 18: Knit to end of row.
Row 19: Purl.
Row 20: Knit.

Ribbons (make two)

Using red 4-ply (fingering) yarn and 2.75mm (UK 12, US 2) knitting needles, cast on 2 sts and knit 1 row.
Next row: K1, M1, K to end of row [3 sts].
Next row: Knit.
Rep last two rows until there are 7 sts.
Continue working in GS until work measures 5cm (2in).
Cast off.

Making up

All pieces of this dog are sewn together with the WS on the outside.

With the WS on the outside, sew up the seam of the body. This will be at the front of the dog. The cast-on edge is at the top. Stuff with toy filling. Fold the base up and pin in place. Sew the base to the body.

With the head shaping forming the top of the head and the cast-off edge forming the back of the head, sew the seam along the bottom of the head and up the front, stuffing it with toy filling as you go.

Next, sew the black-shanked buttons in place as eyes using black sewing cotton. Run the thread from the back of the first eye down to the base of the head and pull slightly, before securing it in place and repeating the process for the second eye. This gives the eyes a more realistic look.

Pin the ears in place on the top of the head and then sew them in place. Use black 4-ply (fingering) yarn to sew the nose to the front of the head; then, using the length of yarn left at the end of the nose, embroider the mouth using straight stitches.

Sew the head to the body using the pictures for guidance on placement.

Sew up the back seam of one front leg and then stuff with toy filling. Repeat for the second leg and pin the legs in place at the front of the body so that the feet touch the floor. Sew up the back seam of the back leg and sew across the cast-off edge, ensuring the back seam is in the middle of the top seam. Repeat for the second back leg. Using the picture for guidance, pin the legs in place just underneath the body towards the back before sewing them in place.

Sew up the side seam of the tail and sew it to the back of the body, placing the seam on top.

Cut a small circle of card to go in the centre of the rosette. Fold the centre of the rosette in half over the card and sew around the edge. Sew the cast-on and cast-off edges of the frill carefully together and pin in place around the centre. Sew the frill to the centre piece. Fold one ribbon in half along the top edge and sew it to the bottom edge of the centre behind the frill. Repeat for the second ribbon, using the picture as guidance. Using black 4-ply (fingering) yarn, embroider the number 1 on the front of the rosette using straight stitches.

Teeny Tiny Doglet

This cheeky tiny doglet is ready to play. His legs are filled with weighting beads making them moveable, so have fun posing him.

Materials
- 46m (50yd) of light brown 4-ply (fingering) yarn
- Small amount of red 4-ply (fingering) yarn
- Toy filling
- Weighting beads
- Black beads: two 4mm (⅛in) and one 6mm (¼in)
- Black sewing cotton and sewing needle
- Two stitch markers
- Stitch holder or spare needle
- Drinking straw (optional)

Needles
2.75mm (UK 12, US 2) knitting needles

Tension
7–8 sts measured over 2.5cm (1in) and worked in SS using 2.75mm (UK 12, US 2) knitting needles and 4-ply (fingering) yarn

Size
9.5cm (3¾in) from top of head to bottom of front legs, and 8cm (3⅛in) from nose to tail

Note
The yarn listed is sufficient to make one of the doglets. For the other doglet, use beige in place of the light brown yarn, and blue in place of the red yarn.

Body and front legs
Start at bottom edge of right foot.
Using light brown 4-ply (fingering) yarn and 2.75mm (UK 12, US 2) knitting needles, cast on 10 sts.
Next row: K2, (Kfb) three times, K5 [13 sts].
Purl 1 row.
Next row: K2, (K2tog) three times, K5 [10 sts].
Work 9 rows in SS.
Next row: Cast off 5 sts, K to end of row [5 sts].
Next row: Cast off 2 sts, P to end of row [3 sts].
Next row: K1, M1, K to end of row [4 sts].
Next row: Cast on 12 sts, P to last st, M1, P1 [17 sts].
Next row: K to last st M1, K1 [18 sts].
Work 19 rows in SS, placing a stitch marker at either end of row 10.
Next row: K to last 3 sts, K2tog, K1 [17 sts].
Next row: P1, P2tog, P to end of row [16 sts].
Knit 1 row.
Next row: Cast off 12 sts, P to end of row [4 sts].
Next row: K1, K2tog, K1 [3 sts].
Next row: Cast on 2 sts, P to end of row [5 sts].
Next row: Cast on 5 sts, K to end of row [10 sts].
Work 9 rows in SS.
Next row: K2, (Kfb) three times, K5 [13 sts].
Purl 1 row.
Next row: K2, (K2tog) three times, K5 [10 sts].
Cast off.

Belly
Using light brown 4-ply (fingering) yarn and 2.75mm (UK 12, US 2) knitting needles, cast on 5 sts and, starting with a knit row, work 6 rows in SS.
Next row: K1, M1, K3, M1, K1 [7 sts].
Work 29 rows in SS.
Next row: K1, ssK, K1, K2tog, K1 [5 sts].
Work 3 rows in SS.
Cast off.

Head

Start at the bottom of the head.

Using light brown 4-ply (fingering) yarn and 2.75mm (UK 12, US 2) knitting needles, cast on 9 sts and, starting with a knit row, work 2 rows in SS. Place these sts on a stitch holder or spare needle.

Using light brown 4-ply (fingering) yarn and 2.75mm (UK 12, US 2) knitting needles, cast on 9 sts and, starting with a knit row, work 2 rows in SS, making the second section.

Next row: With RS facing, knit across 9 sts on needle and then knit across 9 sts on holder or spare needle [18 sts].

Purl 1 row.

Next row: K1, M1, K7, M1, K2, M1, K7, M1, K1 [22 sts].

Next row: P1, M1, P9, M1, P2, M1, P9, M1, P1 [26 sts].

Work 2 rows in SS.

Next row: K10, ssK, K2, K2tog, K10 [24 sts].

Next row: P9, P2tog, P2, P2togtbl, P9 [22 sts].

Next row: K8, ssK, K2, K2tog, K8 [20 sts].

Next row: P7, P2tog, P2, P2togtbl, P7 [18 sts].

Next row: K6, ssK, K2, K2tog, K6 [16 sts].

Purl 1 row.

Next row: K5, ssK, K2, K2tog, K5 [14 sts].

Next row: P1, P2tog, P1, P2togtbl, P2, P2tog, P1, P2togtbl, P1 [10 sts].

Cast off.

Back leg (right)

Using light brown 4-ply (fingering) yarn and 2.75mm (UK 12, US 2) knitting needles, cast on 10 sts.

Next row: K2, (Kfb) three times, K5 [13 sts].

Purl 1 row.

Next row: K2, (K2tog) three times, K5 [10 sts].

Work 9 rows in SS.

Next row: K1, M1, (K3, M1) twice, K3 [13 sts].

Purl 1 row.

Next row: Cast off 9 sts, M1, K3 [5 sts].

Next row: Cast off 2 sts, M1, P1, M1, P1 [5 sts].

* Next row: K1, M1, K to last st, M1, K1 [7 sts].

Next row: P1, M1, P to last st, M1, P1 [9 sts].

Work 4 rows in SS.

Next row: K1, ssK, K to last 3 sts, K2tog, K1 [7 sts].

Next row: P1, P2tog, P1, P2togtbl, P1 [5 sts].

Cast off.

Back leg (left)

Using light brown 4-ply (fingering) yarn and 2.75mm (UK 12, US 2) knitting needles, cast on 10 sts.

Next row: K5, (Kfb) three times, K2 [13 sts].

Purl 1 row.

Next row: K5, (K2tog) three times, K2 [10 sts].

Work 9 rows in SS.

Next row: (K3, M1) three times, K1 [13 sts].

Purl 1 row.

Next row: Cast off 2 sts, M1, K to end of row [12 sts].

Next row: Cast off 9 sts, M1, P1, M1, P1 [5 sts].

Work as for right back leg from * to end.

Ears (make two)

Using light brown 4-ply (fingering) yarn and 2.75mm (UK 12, US 2) knitting needles, cast on 5 sts and, starting with a knit row, work 4 rows in SS.

Next row: SsK, K1, K2tog [3 sts].

Purl 1 row.

Next row: Sl1, K2tog, psso [1 st].

Thread yarn through rem st to fasten, leaving a length of yarn for making up.

Tail

Using light brown 4-ply (fingering) yarn and 2.75mm (UK 12, US 2) knitting needles, cast on 5 sts and, starting with a knit row, work in SS until tail measures 3cm (1¼in), ending with a purl row.

Next row: K1, K2tog, K2 [4 sts].

Work 3 rows in SS.

Thread yarn through sts and fasten, leaving a length of yarn long enough to sew side seam of tail.

Collar

Using red 4-ply (fingering) yarn and 2.75mm (UK 12, US 2) knitting needles, cast on 3 sts and, starting with a knit row, work in SS until collar is long enough to fit around the doglet's neck. Thread yarn through sts and fasten.

Making up

Starting with one of the front legs, thread a length of yarn through the bottom edge of the foot and gather to form the bottom of the foot. Sew the side seam and stuff with weighting beads. You can use a drinking straw to help put the beads inside the narrow leg. Repeat for the second front leg.

Starting with the body, match the middle of the cast-off edge of the belly to the stitch marker at the back of the body, and the middle of the cast-on edge of the belly to the stitch marker at the front of the body. Pin the belly in place. Stuff the body with toy filling and add some weighting beads, sewing the seams of the belly in place.

Sew the cast-off edge of the top of each of the front legs to the belly, using the picture as guidance.

Sew up each back leg in the same way as the front legs (adding weighting beads), then pin the top of the first back leg to the body as shown in the picture. Stuff the top of the leg gently with toy filling and sew it in place, sewing the cast-off edge of the top of the leg to the belly. Repeat for the second back leg.

Fold the cast-off edge of the head in half and sew the stitches together. Sew up the back seam of the head. Stuff gently with toy filling and sew up the bottom seam.

Using a darning needle, take the length of yarn from the last decreased stitch of the ear, run the yarn down the edge stitches on one side of the ear to make the ear bend over. Repeat for the second ear but pull it more tightly to make the ear fold over more, as shown in the picture. Pin the ears in place using the picture as guidance and then sew them firmly in place. Using black sewing cotton, sew the two smaller beads in place for eyes. Sew the larger bead to the front of the face for the nose. Embroider the mouth in place using straight stitches. Sew the head firmly to the front of the body.

Fold the tail in half and sew up the side seam. Fill with a tiny bit of toy filling at the cast-on end. Sew in place using the picture for guidance.

Place the collar around the doglet's neck and carefully sew the cast-on and cast-off edges together.

Sweetheart

Sweetheart just wants to be loved. He is quickly knitted in garter stitch (just knit), which makes him a great project for new knitters wanting to learn some additional skills. He is only tiny, so he will make a great keyring or bag charm.

Materials
35m (38¼yd) of biscuit 10-ply (Aran) yarn
Small amount of dark brown 4-ply (fingering) yarn
Toy filling
Two 6mm (¼in) black beads
Black sewing cotton and sewing needle
Small heart-shaped button
Keyring clasp (optional)

Needles
4mm (UK 8, US 6) knitting needles
2.75mm (UK 12, US 2) knitting needles

Tension
Approximately 16 sts measured over 10cm (4in) and worked in GS using 4mm (UK 8, US 6) knitting needles and 10-ply (Aran) yarn.

Size
9cm (3½in) when sitting down, as shown in the picture opposite

Body
Worked sideways in GS.
Using biscuit 10-ply (Aran) yarn and 4mm (UK 8, US 6) knitting needles, cast on 10 sts and knit 6 rows (GS).
Next row: K6, w&t.
Next row: Knit to end of row.
Work 6 rows in GS.
Next row: K7, w&t.
Next row: K5, w&t.
Next row: K6, w&t.
Next row: K6, w&t.
Next row: K5, w&t.
Next row: Knit to end of row.
Work 6 rows in GS.
Next row: K5, w&t.
Next row: Knit to end of row.
Work 6 rows in GS.
Cast off.

Base
Using biscuit 10-ply (Aran) yarn and 4mm (UK 8, US 6) knitting needles, cast on 6 sts and knit 8 rows (GS).
Next row: K1, (K2tog) twice, K1 [4 sts].
Knit 1 row.
Cast off.

Head

Using biscuit 10-ply (Aran) yarn and 4mm (UK 8, US 6) knitting needles, cast on 14 sts and knit 8 rows (GS).

Next row: K5, (Kfb) four times, K5 [18 sts].

Knit 1 row.

Next row: K5, (Kfb) eight times, K5 [26 sts].

Knit 5 rows.

Next row: K5, (K2tog) eight times, K5 [18 sts].

Knit 1 row.

Next row: K5, (K2tog) four times, K5 [14 sts].

Knit 1 row.

Cast off.

Legs (make two)

Using biscuit 10-ply (Aran) yarn and 4mm (UK 8, US 6) knitting needles, cast on 7 sts and knit 8 rows (GS).

Next row: K3, M1, K1, M1, K3 [9 sts].

Next row: K4, M1, K1, M1, K4 [11 sts].

Next row: K5, M1, K1, M1, K5 [13 sts].

Next row: K6, M1, K1, M1, K6 [15 sts].

Knit 2 rows.

Cast off.

Arms (make two)

Using biscuit 10-ply (Aran) yarn and 4mm (UK 8, US 6) knitting needles cast on 6 sts and knit 8 rows (GS).

Next row: K1, M1, K to last st, M1, K1 [8 sts].

Knit 3 rows.

Next row: (K2tog) four times [4 sts].

Thread yarn through rem sts and fasten.

Ears (make two)

Using 10-ply (Aran) yarn and 4mm (UK 8, US 6) knitting needles, cast on 4 sts and knit 12 rows (GS).

Next row: K1, K2tog, K1 [3 sts].

Cast off.

Tail

Using biscuit 10-ply (Aran) yarn and 4mm (UK 8, US 6) knitting needles, cast on 5 sts and knit 6 rows (GS).

Thread yarn through sts and fasten.

Nose

Worked in SS.

Using dark brown 4-ply (fingering) yarn and 2.75mm (UK 12, US 2) knitting needles, cast on 5 sts and purl 1 row.

Next row: K1, M1, K3, M1, K1 [7 sts].

Work 2 rows in SS.

Next row: P1, P2tog, P1, P2togtbl, P1 [5 sts].

Next row: ssK, K1, K2tog [3 sts].

Cast off.

Making up

Sew the cast-on and cast-off edges of the body together. This forms the back seam. Stuff the body gently with toy filling and sew the base in place with the cast-on edge at the front.

Run a length of yarn through the cast-on edge of the head and gather to form the front of the face. Sew halfway along the seam at the bottom of the head

from front to back. When you are halfway, gather the remaining sts to make the back of the head rounder.

Pin the ears to the top of the head and sew them in place. Pin the nose to the front of the head using the picture for guidance and sew it in place.

Use black sewing cotton and a sewing needle to sew the black beads in place for eyes at the start of the head shaping.

Pin the head on to the body, matching the back seam of the head to the back seam of the body. Sew in place, using the picture for guidance.

Sew up the back seam of the first leg, stuffing it gently with toy filling as you go. Sew the seam along the base of the foot. Repeat for the second leg, then pin them both in place, using the picture for guidance, before sewing them in place.

Sew up the seam of the arm, stuffing gently with toy filling as you go. Repeat for the second arm, then pin them both in place, using the picture for guidance, and placing the seam towards the bottom. Sew the arms in place.

Fold the tail in half lengthways and sew it together. Sew it in place at the back of the dog using the picture for guidance.

Sew the heart-shaped button to the front of the dog using biscuit 10-ply (Aran) yarn to finish.

Optionally, you might like to use biscuit 10-ply (Aran) yarn to sew a keyring clasp to the back of the dog, just below the head, as shown below.

Labrador

You might like to give this little labrador away as a gift – he is bound to be loved wherever he goes. Of course, if you can't bear to be parted from this chubby, cuddly chap, keep him for yourself! A big bow made from ribbon sets him off nicely.

Materials
115m (126yd) of mustard 10-ply (Aran) yarn
Small amount of black 4-ply (fingering) yarn
Two 8mm (⅜in) black shanked buttons
Toy filling
Red ribbon, 60cm (23½in)

Needles
4mm (UK 8, US 6) knitting needles
2.75mm (UK 12, US 2) knitting needles

Tension
4–5 sts measured over 2.5cm (1in) and worked in SS using 4mm (UK 8, US 6) knitting needles and 10-ply (Aran) yarn

Size
21cm (8¼in) from nose to tail, and 18cm (7in) from top of the head to the bottom of the feet

Body
Using mustard 10-ply (Aran) yarn and 4mm (UK 8, US 6) knitting needles, cast on 14 sts and purl 1 row.
Next row: K1, (Kfb, K1, Kfb) to last st, K1.
Next row: Purl 1 row [22 sts].
Next row: K1, (Kfb, K3, Kfb) to last st, K1.
Next row: Purl 1 row [30 sts].
Next row: K1, (Kfb, K5, Kfb) to last st, K1.
Next row: Purl 1 row [38 sts].
Next row: K1, (Kfb, K7, Kfb) to last st, K1.
Next row: Purl 1 row [46 sts].
Work 26 rows in SS.

Next row: K1, ssK, K17, K2tog, K2, ssK, K17, K2tog, K1 [42 sts].
Purl 1 row.
Next row: K1, ssK, K15, K2tog, K2, ssK, K15, K2tog, K1 [38 sts].
Next row: P1, P2tog, P13, P2togtbl, P2, P2tog, P13, P2togtbl, P1 [34 sts].
Next row: K1, ssK, K11, K2tog, K2, ssK, K11, K2tog, K1 [30 sts].
Next row: P1, P2tog, P9, P2togtbl, P2, P2tog, P9, P2togtbl, P1 [26 sts].
Next row: K1, ssK, K7, K2tog, K2, ssK, K7, K2tog, K1 [22 sts].
Cast off using three needle cast off technique (see page 13).

Head
Using mustard 10-ply (Aran) yarn and 4mm (UK 8, US 6) knitting needles, cast on 14 sts and purl 1 row.
Next row: K1, M1, K to last st, M1, K1 [16 sts].
Next row: P1, M1, P to last st, M1, P1 [18 sts].
Rep last two rows twice more [26 sts].
Next row: K1, M1, K to last st, M1, K1 [28 sts].
Purl 1 row.
Next row: K13, M1, K2, M1, K13 [30 sts].
Next row: P14, M1, P2, M1, P14 [32 sts].
Next row: K15, M1, K2, M1, K15 [34 sts].
Next row: P16, M1, P2, M1, P16 [36 sts].
Next row: K17, M1, K2, M1, K17 [38 sts].
Next row: P18, M1, P2, M1, P18 [40 sts].
Next row: K19, M1, K2, M1, K19 [42 sts].
Work 7 rows in SS.
Next row: K1, ssK, K15, K2tog, K2, ssK, K15, K2tog, K1 [38 sts].
Purl 1 row.

Next row: K1, ssK, K13, K2tog, K2, ssK, K13, K2tog, K1 [34 sts].

Next row: P1, P2tog, P11, P2togtbl, P2, P2tog, P11, P2togtbl, P1 [30 sts].

Next row: K1, ssK, K9, K2tog, K2, ssK, K9, K2tog, K1 [26 sts].

Next row: P1, P2tog, P7, P2togtbl, P2, P2tog, P7, P2togtbl, P1 [22 sts].

Next row: K1, ssK, K5, K2tog, K2, ssK, K5, K2tog, K1 [18 sts].

Cast off using the three needle cast off technique (see page 13).

Left legs (make two)

Using mustard 10-ply (Aran) yarn and 4mm (UK 8, US 6) knitting needles, cast on 6 sts and purl 1 row.

Continuing in SS, cast on 2 sts at the beginning of the next 4 rows [14 sts].

Work 2 rows in SS.

Next row: K1, M1, K to last st, M1, K1 [16 sts].

Work 5 rows in SS.

Next row: K2, (Kfb) five times, K9 [21 sts].

Work 4 rows in SS.

Next row: P9, (P2tog) five times, P2 [16 sts].

Next row: (K2tog) eight times [8 sts].

Purl 1 row.

Next row: (K2tog) four times [4 sts].

Thread yarn through remaining sts and fasten.

Right legs (make two)

Using mustard 10-ply (Aran) yarn and 4mm (UK 8, US 6) knitting needles, cast on 6 sts and purl 1 row.

Continuing in SS, cast on 2 sts at the beginning of the next 4 rows [14 sts].

Work 2 rows in SS.

Next row: K1, M1, K to last st, M1, K1 [16 sts].

Work 5 rows in SS.

Next row: K9, (Kfb) five times, K2 [21 sts].

Work 4 rows in SS.

Next row: P2, (P2tog) five times, P9 [16 sts].

Next row: (K2tog) eight times [8 sts].

Purl 1 row.

Next row: (K2tog) four times [4 sts].

Thread yarn through remaining sts and fasten.

Nose

Using black 4-ply (fingering) yarn and 2.75mm (UK 12, US 2) knitting needles, cast on 7 sts and, starting with a knit row, work 5 rows in SS.

Next row: P2tog, P to last 2 sts, P2tog [5 sts].

Next row: K2tog, K1, K2tog [3 sts].

Next row: Sl1, P2tog, psso [1 st].

Fasten off rem st, leaving a length of yarn long enough to embroider the mouth.

Ears (make four)

Cast on 8 sts using mustard 10-ply (Aran) yarn and 4mm (UK 8, US 6) knitting needles and, starting with a knit row, work 6 rows in SS.

Next row: K1, M1, K to last st, M1, K1 [10 sts].

Work 5 rows in SS.

Next row: K1, M1, K to last st, M1, K1 [12 sts].

Work 3 rows in SS.

Next row: K1, ssK, K to last 3 sts, K2tog, K1 [10 sts].

Next row: P1, P2tog, P to last 3 sts, P2togtbl, P1 [8 sts].

Cast off.

Tail

Cast on 12 sts using mustard 10-ply (Aran) yarn and 4mm (UK 8, US 6) knitting needles and, starting with a knit row, work 8 rows in SS.

Next row: K1, ssK, K to last 3 sts, K2tog, K1 [10 sts].

Purl 1 row.

Rep last two rows three more times [4 sts].

Thread yarn through rem sts and fasten, leaving a length of yarn long enough to sew the side seam of the tail.

Making up

Starting at the cast-off end of the body, sew the seam and stuff with toy filling. Gather the cast-on edge and fasten. Sew the head together in the same way, up to the nose. To finish the head, gather the nose following the instructions on page 13.

Place two ear pieces with WS together and sew around the edges to make one ear. Repeat for the second ear. Pin the ears in place on either side of the centre four stitches on the top of the head. Sew in place. Sew black-shanked buttons in place as eyes and run a length of yarn from the back of each eye to the bottom of the head, pulling the yarn and securing. This gives the face a realistic look. Sew the nose in place using black 4-ply (fingering) and embroider the mouth using straight stitches and the length of yarn left at the end of the nose. Place the head at the cast-off end of the body, using the picture as guidance and sew in place.

Gather the yarn at the bottom of the foot and sew the base of one foot and the side seam of the leg. Stuff with toy filling, then repeat for other three legs. Pin the legs in place on the body, using the picture as guidance. The legs are shaped to fit on the curved sides of the body so take care to make sure they are on the correct side.

Sew the side seam of the tail. Stuff with toy filling. Pin the tail in place with the seam facing towards the top of the dog, then sew it in place.

Tie a ribbon into a bow around the dog's neck.

Bonnie Prince Charlie

Charlie is inspired by a lovely King Charles Spaniel of the same name who was very loved by his owner. I hope my Charlie does him justice. By using a 'loopy' stitch you get a fabulous fluffy look. Just do not try to take his sausages from him!

Materials
35m (38¼yd) of cream 5-ply (sportweight) yarn
56m (61¼yd) of brown 5-ply (sportweight) yarn
Small amounts of black, blue and gold 4-ply (fingering) yarn
Toy filling
Chenille sticks
Two 6mm (¼in) black beads
Black sewing cotton and sewing needle
Stitch markers
Spare needle or stitch holder

Needles
2.75mm (UK 12, US 2) knitting needles
3.25mm (UK 10, US 3) knitting needles

Tension
5–6 sts to 2.5cm (1in) measured over SS using 3.25mm (UK 10, US 3) knitting needles

Size
11cm (4⅜in) tall and 13cm (5⅛in) long, excluding the tail

Body and front legs
Start at right front foot.
Using cream 5-ply (sportweight) yarn and 3.25mm (UK 10, US 3) knitting needles, cast on 10 sts and knit 1 row.
Next row: P8, turn.
Next row: K3, turn.
Next row: P3, turn.
Next row: K3, turn.
Next row: P5 (to end of row).

Next row: K2, K3B, K5.
Work 5 rows in SS.
Next row: K6, M1, K3, M1, K1 [12 sts].
Work 2 rows in SS.
Cast off 1 st at the beg of the next row (WS) [11 sts].
Next row: Cast off 5 sts, K1, change to brown 5-ply (sportweight) yarn, K4 [6 sts].
Next row: Cast on 12 sts, P16 in brown, P2 in cream [18 sts].
Next row: K1, M1 in cream, change to brown, K16, M1, K1 [20 sts].
From now on use brown 5-ply (sportweight) yarn only for the body.
Purl 1 row.
Next row: K to last st, M1, K1 [21 sts].
Purl 1 row.
Work 20 rows in SS, placing a marker at the beg and end of row 10.
Next row: K to last 3 sts, K2tog, K1 [20 sts].
P18 using brown yarn, join in cream yarn, P2.
Next row: K3 in cream, change to brown, K to last 3 sts, K2tog, K1 [19 sts].
Cast off 13 sts, P2, change to cream, P3 [6 sts].
Cast on 5 sts, K8, change to brown, K3 [11 sts].
From now on use cream yarn only.
Cast on 1 st at the beg of the next row [12 sts].
Work 2 rows in SS.
Next row: K5, K2tog, K2, ssK, K1 [10 sts].
Work 6 rows in SS.
Next row: P8, turn.
Next row: K3, turn.
Next row: P3, turn.
Next row: K3, turn.
Next row: P5 (to end of row).
Next row: K2, K3B, K5.
Cast off rem 10 sts.

Belly

Loopy stitch: Knit into the stitch and keep the stitch on the needle instead of transferring it to the other needle. Bring the working yarn towards you between the needles. Place your thumb on the yarn and wrap the yarn around your thumb to make a loop. Pass the yarn back between the two needles, making the loop at the front of the work. Keeping the yarn wrapped around your thumb, knit into the same stitch again. Let the stitch fall off your needle and take the loop off your thumb. You now have two stitches on your right-hand needle instead of one and a loop. Knit these two stitches together to make one stitch and secure the loop.

The belly is worked in loopy stitch. All RS rows are worked in loopy stitch and WS rows are purled.

Using cream 5-ply (sportweight) yarn and 3.25mm (UK 10, US 3) knitting needles, cast on 3 sts and, starting with a knit row, work 4 rows in SS.

Next row: K1, M1, K to last st, M1, K1 [5 sts].

Work 3 rows.

Rep the last 4 rows once more [7 sts].

Work 12 rows.

Next row: K2tog, K3, K2tog [5 sts].

Work 3 rows.

Next row: K2tog, K1, K2tog [3 sts].

Work 10 rows. Cast off.

Head

The head is worked from the 'chin' of the dog. A right and left section are worked and then joined together to knit the rest of the head.

Right side

Using cream 5-ply (sportweight) yarn and 3.25mm (UK 10, US 3) knitting needles, cast on 5 sts and knit 1 row.

From now on work all sts marked in **bold** using brown 5-ply (sportweight) yarn and all other sts in cream.

Cast on 4 sts at beginning of next row in brown, P5, P3, M1, P1 [10 sts].

Next row: K1, M1, K3, **K4**, **M1**, **K2** [12 sts].

Next row: **P8**, P3, M1, P1 [13 sts].

Cut yarn and place sts on a spare needle/stitch holder.

Left side

Using cream yarn and 3.25mm (UK 10, US 3) knitting needles cast on 5 sts and P 1 row.

Next row: **Cast on 4 sts**, **K5**, K3, M1, K1 [10 sts].

Next row: P1, M1, P3, **P5**, **M1**, **P1** [12 sts].

Next row: **K8**, K3, M1, K1 [13 sts].

Cut the yarn and from now on work only in brown 5-ply (sportweight) yarn.

With RS facing and the cream sts in the middle, place the two sections on to one needle. With RS facing and using brown 5-ply (sportweight) yarn, and starting with a knit row, work 2 rows in SS [26 sts].

Next row: K10, ssK, K2, K2tog, K10 [24 sts].

Next row: P9, P2tog, P2, P2togtbl, P9 [22 sts].

Next row: K8, ssK, K2, K2tog, K8 [20 sts].

Next row: P7, P2tog, P2, P2togtbl, P7 [18 sts].

Work 2 rows in SS.

Next row: K1, ssK, K to last 3 sts, K2tog, K1 [16 sts].

Next row: P1, P2tog, P to last 3 sts, P2togtbl, P1 [14 sts].

Cast off 4 sts at the beginning of the next two rows [6 sts].

Work 8 rows in SS.

Next row: K1, ssK, K2tog, K1 [4 sts].

Work 3 rows in SS.

Next row: ssK, K2tog.

Next row: P2tog.

Fasten off remaining st.

Back leg (left)

Using cream 5-ply (sportweight) yarn and 3.25mm (UK 10, US 3) knitting needles, cast on 10 sts and knit 1 row.

Next row: P5, turn.

Next row: K3, turn.

Next row: P3, turn.

Next row: K3, turn.

P8 (to end of row).

Next row: K5, K3B, K2.

Purl 1 row.

Next row: K6, join in brown 5-ply (sportweight) yarn and K4 in brown.

Next row: P6 in brown, P4 in cream.

Next row: K3 in cream, K7 in brown.

From now on use only brown 5-ply (sportweight) yarn and purl 1 row.

Next row: K4, w&t.

Next row: P3, w&t.

Next row: K3, w&t.

Next row: P4 (to end of row).

Next row: (K1, M1), twice, K3, M1, K1, M1, K4 [14 sts].

Purl 1 row.

Next row: K2, M1, K1, M1, K5, M1, K1, M1, K5 [18 sts].

Purl 1 row.

Next row: Cast off 3 sts, M1, K to last st, M1, K1 [17 sts].

Next row: Cast off 6 sts, M1, P to last st, M1, P1 [13 sts].

Work 4 rows in SS.

Next row: K1, ssK, K to last 3 sts, K2tog, K1 [11 sts].

Next row: P1, P2tog, P to last 3 sts, P2togtbl, P1 [9 sts].

Rep the last two rows once more [5 sts].

Cast off rem sts.

Back leg (right)

Using cream 5-ply (sportweight) yarn and 3.25mm (UK 10, US 3) knitting needles, cast on 10 sts and knit 1 row.

Next row: P8, turn.

Next row: K3, turn.

Next row: P3, turn.

Next row: K3, turn.

P5 (to end of row).

Next row: K2, K3B, K5.

Purl 1 row.

Next row: Join in brown 5-ply (sportweight) yarn, K4, K6 in cream.

Next row: P5 in cream, P5 in brown.

Next row: K7 in brown, K3 in cream.

From now on use only brown 5-ply (sportweight) yarn.

Purl 1 row.

Next row: K9, w&t.

Next row: P3, w&t.

Next row: K3, w&t.

Next row: P9 (to end of row).

Next row: K4, M1, K1, M1, K3, (M1, K1) twice [14 sts].

Purl 1 row.

Next row: K5, M1, K1, M1, K5, M1, K1, M1, K2 [18 sts].

Purl 1 row.

Next row: Cast off 6 sts, M1, K to last st, M1, K1 [14 sts].

Next row: Cast off 3 sts, M1, P to last st, M1, K1 [13 sts].

Work 4 rows in SS.

Next row: K1, ssK, K to last 3 sts, K2tog, K1 [11 sts].

Next row: P1, P2tog, P to last 3 sts, P2togtbl, P1 [9 sts].

Rep the last two rows once more.

Cast off rem 5 sts.

Tail

All RS rows are worked in loopy stitch (see opposite) and WS rows are purled. Using brown 5-ply (sportweight) yarn and 3.25mm (UK 10, US 3) knitting needles cast on 7 sts. Starting with a knit row, work 4.5cm (1¾in) in SS, ending with a purl row.

Next row: K2, K2tog, K3 [6 sts].

Work 3 rows in SS.

Change to cream 5-ply (sportweight) yarn and work 3 rows in SS.

Thread yarn through sts and fasten.

Ears (make two)

Cast on 5 sts using brown 5-ply (sportweight) yarn and 3.25mm (UK 10, US 3) knitting needles and, starting with a knit row, work 6 rows in SS.

Next row: K1, M1, K to last st, M1, K1 [7 sts].

Work 3 rows in SS.

Rep last four rows once more [9 sts].

Next row: K1, ssK, K3, K2tog, K1 [7 sts].

Next row: P1, P2tog, P1, P2togtbl, P1 [5 sts].

Purl 1 row. (This row forms a fold-line.)

Next row: P1, M1, P to last st, M1, P1 [7 sts].

Next row: K1, M1, K to last st, M1, K1 [9 sts].

Work 3 rows in SS.

Next row: K1, ssK, K3, K2tog, K1 [7 sts].

Work 3 rows in SS.

Next row: K1, ssK, K1, K2tog, K1 [5 sts].

Work 6 rows in SS.

Cast off.

Front face section

Cast on 10 sts using cream 5-ply (sportweight) yarn and 3.25mm (UK 10, US 3) knitting needles and purl 1 row.

Next row: K1, M1, K to last st, M1, K1 [12 sts].

Next row: P1, M1, P to last st, M1, P1 [14 sts].

Knit 1 row.

Next row: P1, P2tog, P to last 3 sts, P2togtbl, P1 [12 sts].

Next row: K1, K2tog, K to last 3 sts, ssK, K1 [10 sts].

Next row: P2tog, cast off 2 sts, P to end of row [7 sts].

Next row: K2tog, cast off 2 sts, K to end of row [4 sts].

Next row: (P2tog) twice [2 sts].

Work 2 rows in SS.

Next row: K1, M1, K1 [3 sts].

Purl 1 row.

Next row: (K1, M1) twice, K1 [5 sts].

Work 6 rows in SS.

Next row: P2tog, P1, P2togtbl [3 sts].

Next row: Sl1, K2tog, psso [1 st].

Fasten off remaining st.

Eyebrows (make two)

Cast on 4 sts using brown 5-ply (sportweight) yarn and 3.25mm (UK 10, US 3) knitting needles and knit 1 row.

Next row: P3, turn.

Next row: K2, turn.

Next row: P3 (to end of row).

Cast off.

Nose

Cast on 1 st using black 4-ply (fingering) yarn and 2.75mm (UK 12, US 2) knitting needles.

Next row: Kfbf [3 sts].

Next row: (K1, M1) twice, K1 [5 sts].

Work 4 rows in SS.

Next row: P2tog, P1, P2tog [3 sts].

Next row: Sl1, K2tog, psso [1 st].

Fasten off rem st.

Collar

Using blue 4-ply (fingering) yarn and 2.75mm (UK 12, US 2) knitting needles, cast on 4 sts and work in SS until collar fits around dog's neck. Cast off.

Note: This can also be worked on double-pointed needles as an i-cord.

Dog tag

Using gold 4-ply (fingering) yarn and 2.75mm (UK 12, US 2) knitting needles cast on 4 st and knit 1 row.

Next row: K1, M1, K2, M1, K1 [6 sts].

Knit 2 rows.

Next row: K1, ssK, K2tog, K1 [4 sts].

Knit 1 row.

Cast off.

Making up

Sew the side seams of the back gusset of the head and then sew the chin and bottom of the head together. The chin is the cream part of the head. Lightly stuff with toy filling to shape the head. Take the cream front face section, which is roughly a 'T' shape. Fold approximately three rows of the cast-on edge under and sew in place. Pin the face section in place so that the cast-on edge is overlapping the cream nose and the narrower part is on the top of the head. Sew in place. The picture on page 103 shows this well.

Run a length of yarn around the nose, gather and then sew to the front edge of the face section where it joins the main part of the head. Using black sewing cotton, sew the black beads in place as eyes, as shown in the photographs. Pull a thread from each eye to the base of the head and tighten, pulling the eyes in. This gives the head a realistic shape.

Sew the cast-on edge of one eyebrow to the cast-off edge. Repeat for the second eyebrow, then sew both in place above each eye. Sew the side and top seams of the ears and sew to the top of the head, either side of the cream section.

Starting with one of the front legs, thread a length of yarn through the bottom edge of the foot and gather to form the bottom of the foot. Sew the side seam and stuff with toy filling, placing a chenille stick inside the toy filling. Repeat for the second front leg.

Matching the middle of the cast-off edge of the belly to the stitch marker at the back of the body, and the middle of the cast-on edge of the belly to the stitch marker at the front of the body, pin the belly in place. Stuff the body firmly with toy filling, sewing the seams of the belly in place. Sew the cast-off edge of the top of each front leg to the belly.

Thread a chenille stick through the bottom of the body and slide each end down inside the front legs. Gather the end of one foot into a circle by running a thread through the stitches and sew the side seam of the leg. Stuff and sew the top of the leg to the belly. Repeat for the second front leg and foot.

Sew the foot and leg seams of the back legs as described for the front legs and sew them to the body. Place a length of chenille stick inside each leg, stuff gently and sew the top of the leg to the body, using the pictures as guidance, and sliding the chenille stick into the body to avoid sharp ends protruding.

Sew the ends of yarn in on the tail, slide a length of chenille stick inside and sew it to the back of the body as shown. Sew the cast-on and cast-off edges of the collar together around the dog's neck. Sew the dog tag to the front of the collar.

Cuddle Pup

Cuddle pup is super-easy to knit and makes great use of the colour changing wool available. He has his arms out for a cuddle and would be a great project for a new knitter – just remember to give him his quirky embroidered smile for the perfect finishing touch.

Materials
- 140m (153yd) of 12-ply (chunky) yarn
- Small amount of 10-ply (Aran) yarn for the ear linings
- Small amount of black 4-ply (fingering) yarn for the nose
- Toy filling
- Two 8mm (⅜in) black shanked buttons
- Black sewing cotton and sewing needle

Needles
- 2.75mm (UK 12, US 2) knitting needles
- 4.5mm (UK 7, US 7) knitting needles
- 5.5mm (UK 5, US 9) knitting needles

Tension
13 sts measured over 10cm (4in) and worked in SS using 5.5mm (UK 5, US 9) knitting needles and 12-ply (chunky) yarn

Size
24cm (9½in) from top of head to bottom.

Body (make two)
Using 12-ply (chunky) yarn and 5.5mm (UK 5, US 9) knitting needles, cast on 26 sts and, starting with a knit row, work 2 rows in SS.
Next row: K1, M1, K to last st, M1, K1 [28 sts].
Purl 1 row.
Rep last two rows twice more [32 sts].
Work 22 rows in SS.
Next row: K1, ssK, K to last 3 sts, K2tog, K1 [30 sts].
Work 3 rows in SS.
Rep last four rows twice more [26 sts].
Next row: K1, ssK, K to last 3 sts, K2tog, K1 [24 sts].
Purl 1 row.
Rep last two rows three times more [18 sts].
Next row: K1, ssK, K to last 3 sts, K2tog, K1 [16 sts].
Next row: P1, P2tog, P to last 3 sts, P2togtbl, P1 [14 sts].
Next row: K1, ssK, K to last 3 sts, K2tog, K1 [12 sts].
Cast off.

Base
Using 12-ply (chunky) yarn and 5.5mm (UK 5, US 9) knitting needles, cast on 10 sts and purl 1 row.
Next row: K1, M1, K to last st, M1, K1 [12 sts].
Next row: P1, M1, P to last st, M1, P1 [14 sts].
Rep last two rows twice more [22 sts].
Work 4 rows in SS.
Next row: K1, ssK, K to last 3 sts, K2tog, K1 [20 sts].
Next row: P1, P2tog, P to last 3 sts, P2togtbl, P1 [18 sts].
Rep last two rows twice more [10 sts].
Knit 1 row.
Cast off.

Snout

Using 12-ply (chunky) yarn and 5.5mm (UK 5, US 9) knitting needles, cast on 20 sts and purl 1 row.

Next row: K1, ssK, K to last 3 sts, K2tog, K1 [18 sts].

Next row: P1, P2tog, P to last 3 sts, P2togtbl, P1 [16 sts].

Rep last two rows once more [12 sts].

Rep first row once more [10 sts].

Cast off.

Ears (make two)

Using 12-ply (chunky) yarn and 5.5mm (UK 5, US 9) knitting needles, cast on 8 sts and, starting with a knit row, work 4 rows in SS.

Next row: K1, M1, K to last st, M1, K1 [10 sts].

Work 9 rows in SS.

Next row: K1, ssK, K to last 3 sts, K2tog, K1 [8 sts].

Next row: P1, P2tog, P to last 3 sts, P2togtbl, P1 [6 sts].

Cast off.

Ear linings (make two)

Using 10-ply (Aran) yarn and 4.5mm (UK 7, US 7) knitting needles, cast on 8 sts and, starting with a knit row, work 6 rows in SS.

Next row: K1, M1, K to last st, M1, K1 [10 sts].

Work 7 rows in SS.

Next row: K1, ssK, K to last 3 sts, K2tog, K1 [8 sts].

Purl 1 row.

Rep last two rows once more [6 sts].

Cast off.

Nose

Using black 4-ply (fingering) yarn and 2.75mm (UK 12, US 2) knitting needles, cast on 3 sts and purl 1 row.

Next row: K1, M1, K to last st, M1, K1 [5 sts].

Purl 1 row.

Rep last two rows once more [7 sts].

Work 2 rows in SS.

Next row: K1, ssK, K1, K2tog, K1 [5 sts].

Cast off.

Arms (make two)

Using 12-ply (chunky) yarn and 5.5mm (UK 5, US 9) knitting needles, cast on 14 sts and, starting with a knit row, work 12 rows in SS.

Next row: K1, ssK, K1, K2tog, K2, ssK, K1, K2tog, K1 [10 sts].

Purl 1 row.

Cast off.

Feet (make two)

Using 12-ply (chunky) yarn and 5.5mm (UK 5, US 9) knitting needles, cast on 16 sts and, starting with a knit row, work 6 rows in SS.

Next row: K1, ssK, K2, K2tog, K2, ssK, K2, K2tog, K1 [12 sts].

Purl 1 row.

Cast off.

Tail

Using 12-ply (chunky) yarn and 5.5mm (UK 5, US 9) knitting needles, cast on 10 sts and, starting with a knit row, work 10 rows in SS.

Next row: (K2tog) five times [5 sts].

Thread yarn through rem sts and fasten.

Making up

Sew the body pieces together and stuff them gently with toy filling. The cast-on edges are at the bottom. Pin and sew the base in place. Fold the cast-off edge of the snout in half and sew the cast-off stitches together. Sew up the shaped seam, then pin it in place on the body with the seam underneath, using the picture for guidance. Stuff gently with toy filling and sew in place.

Fold the arm in half and sew up the side seam. Stuff gently with toy filling and sew the cast-on edges together. Repeat for the second arm. Pin the arms in place on the body at a slight angle and sew in place using the picture for guidance and placing the seams towards the bottom.

Fold the foot in half and sew up the side seam. Stuff gently with toy filling and sew the cast-on edges together. Repeat for the second foot. Pin the feet in place along the bottom seam of the body and base, then sew them in place.

Fold the tail in half and sew up the side seam. Stuff it with a small amount of toy filling. Sew the tail in place approximately 3cm (1⅛in) up from the bottom of the back.

With WS together, pin and sew the ear lining to the ear, then repeat for the second ear. Pin the ears in place at a slight angle at the top of the head using the picture as guidance, then sew them in place.

Sew the nose to the front of the snout with the cast-off edge at the top and embroider the mouth using straight stitches and black 4-ply (fingering) yarn, using the picture for guidance. Using black sewing cotton, sew the black shanked buttons in place for the eyes above the snout, approximately four stitches apart as shown opposite.

Doggy Treats

Every good dog deserves a treat now and again. The large bowl doubles as a tiny bed for the smaller dogs, so you even have somewhere to send them if they have been naughty!

Bones

Each bone is worked using the same pattern and cream 4-ply (fingering) yarn. For small bones, use a single strand of yarn and 2.75mm (UK 12, US 2) needles. For large bones, use a double strand of yarn and 4mm (UK 8, US 6) needles.

Bone

Cast on 12 sts and purl 1 row.
Next row: K1, M1, K4, M1, K2, M1, K4, M1, K1 [16 sts].
Next row: P1, M1, P6, M1, P2, M1, P6, M1, P1 [20 sts].
Knit 1 row.
Next row: P1, P2tog, P4, P2togtbl, P2, P2tog, P4, P2togtbl, P1 [16 sts].
Next row: K1, ssK, K2, K2tog, K2, ssK, K2, K2tog, K1 [12 sts].
Next row: P1, P2tog, P2togtbl, P2, P2tog, P2togtbl, P1 [8 sts].
Starting with a knit row, work 8 rows in SS.
Next row: K1, M1, K2, M1, K2, M1, K2, M1, K1 [12 sts].
Next row: P1, M1, P4, M1, P2, M1, P4, M1, P1 [16 sts].
Next row: K1, M1, K6, M1, K2, M1, K6, M1, K1 [20 sts].
Purl 1 row.
Next row: K1, K2tog, K4, K2togtbl, K2, K2tog, K4, K2togtbl, K1 [16 sts].
Next row: P1, P2tog, P2, P2togtbl, P2, P2tog, P2, P2togtbl, P1 [12 sts].
Knit 1 row.
Cast off.

Making up

Fold in half lengthwise and sew the cast-off edge together. Sew the side seam, stuffing with toy filling as you go. Sew along the top (cast-on) edge of the bone. Using a cream 4-ply (fingering) yarn, sew a stitch over the middle of each end of the bone, approximately 4–5 sts down from the edge on either side, pull tight and secure. This will make a great shape at both ends of the bone. Use the picture for guidance.

Materials

Small amount of cream 4-ply (fingering) yarn
75m (82yd) of royal blue 4-ply (fingering) yarn
16m (17½yd) of turquoise 4-ply (fingering) yarn
Small amount of brown 10-ply (Aran) yarn
Toy filling

Needles

2.75mm (UK 12, US 2) knitting needles
4mm (UK 8, US 6) knitting needles

Tension

Large bone: 3–4 sts measured over 2.5cm (1in) and worked in SS using 4mm (UK 8, US 6) knitting needles and a double strand of 4-ply (fingering) yarn.
Small bone: 7–8 sts measured over 2.5cm (1in) and worked in SS using 2.75mm (UK 12, US 2) knitting needles and 4-ply (fingering) yarn.

Size

Large bone: 7.5cm (3in) long; small bone: 5cm (2in) long.
Large bowl 7.5cm (3in) in diameter; small bowl 4cm (1½in) in diameter.
Each sausage is approximately 3cm (1¼in) long.

Large bowl

Base

Using a double strand of royal blue 4-ply (fingering) yarn and 4mm (UK 8, US 6) needles, cast on 7 sts.
Next row: K1, M1, K to last st, M1, K1 [9 sts].
Knit 1 row.
Next row: K1, M1, K to last st, M1, K1 [11 sts].
Rep last row a further five times [21 sts].
Work 16 rows in GS.
Next row: K1, K2tog, K to last 3 sts, K2tog, K1 [19 sts].
Rep last row a further five times [9 sts].
Knit 1 row.
Next row: K1, K2tog, K to last 3 sts, K2tog, K1 [7 sts].
Cast off.

Side

Using a double strand of royal blue 4-ply (fingering) yarn and 4mm (UK 8, US 6) needles, cast on 8 sts and work in GS until side of bowl is long enough to go all around the base.

Cast off.

Paw print decoration

Using a single strand of 4-ply (fingerring) yarn and using 2.75mm (UK 12, US 2) needles, cast on 5 sts and purl 1 row.

Next row: K1, M1, K to last st, M1, K1 [7 sts].

Purl 1 row.

Cast off 2 sts at the beg of the next two rows [3 sts].

Work 2 rows in SS.

Next row: Sl1, K2tog, psso [1 st].

Fasten off rem st.

Making up

Using royal blue 4-ply (fingering) yarn, sew one long edge of the side of the bowl to the base and then sew up remaining seam. Using cream yarn sew the paw in place and sew four French knots for the pads.

Small bowl

Base

Using a single strand of turquoise 4-ply (fingering) yarn and 2.75mm (UK 12, US 2) needles, cast on 7 sts.

Next row: K1, M1, K to last st, M1, K1 [9 sts].

Knit 1 row.

Next row: K1, M1, K to last st, M1, K1 [11 sts].

Rep last row a further five times [21 sts].

Work 16 rows in GS.

Next row: K1, K2tog, K to last 3 sts, K2tog, K1 [19 sts].

Rep last row a further five times [9 sts].

Knit 1 row.

Next row: K1, K2tog, K to last 3 sts, K2tog, K1 [7 sts].

Cast off.

Side

Using turquoise 4-ply (fingering) yarn and 2.75mm (UK 12, US 2) needles, cast on 5 sts and work in GS until the side of the bowl is long enough to go all around the base.

Cast off.

Bone decoration

Using cream 4-ply (fingering) yarn and 2.75mm (UK 12, US 2) needles, cast on 5 sts and purl 1 row.

Next row: K1, M1, K to last st, M1, K1 [7 sts].

Purl 1 row.

Cast off 2 sts at the beginning of the next two rows [3 sts].

Work 2 rows in SS.

Next row: K1, M1, K to last st, M1, K1 [5 sts].

Purl 1 row.

Rep last two rows once more [7 sts].

Next row: K1, ssK, K1, K2tog, K1 [5 sts].

Cast off.

Making up

Using turquoise 4-ply (fingering) yarn, sew one long edge of the side of the bowl to the base and then sew up remaining seam. Using cream 4-ply (fingering) yarn, sew the bone in place, tucking the cast-on and cast-off edges under to make it neat.

String of sausages

Using brown 10-ply (Aran) yarn and 4mm (UK 8, US 6) knitting needles, cast on 5 sts.

* **Next row:** (K1, M1) four times, K1 [9 sts].

Starting with a purl row, work 7 rows in SS.

Next row: (K2tog) twice, K1, (K2tog) twice [5 sts].

Purl 1 row. *

Rep from * to * five more times. Thread through rem stitches and fasten.

Making up

Sew along seams of sausages, stuffing with toy filling as you go. Sew tightly around the join between each sausage to add definition.

Abbreviations

beg	beginning
CC	**contrast colour**
cm	centimetres
C4F	Slip the next two stitches on to a cable needle and hold at the front of the work. Knit the following two stitches and then knit the two stitches from the cable needle
foll	following
GS	garter stitch
in	inch
K	knit
K2tog	knit 2 stitches together
K2togtbl	knit 2 stitches together through the backs of the loops.
K3B	pass next stitch to RH needle, pick up stitch 3 rows below and knit together with this stitch. Repeat for next two stitches. This creates a 'fold' in the knitting.
Kfb	knit into front and back of stitch (increasing one stitch)
Kfbf	knit into the front, back and front of the stitch (increasing two stitches)
M	marker
M1	make a backwards loop on your needle by twisting the yarn towards you and slipping the resulting loop on to the right-hand needle. On the following row, knit or purl through the back of the stitch. This produces a very neat result.
MC	Main colour
P	purl
P2tog	purl 2 stitches together
P2togtbl	purl 2 stitches together through the backs of the loops.
P3B	pass next stitch to RH needle, pick up stitch 3 rows below and purl together with this stitch. Repeat for the next two stitches.
Pfb	Purl into front and back of stitch (increasing one stitch)
PM	place marker
psso	pass slipped stitch over
rem	remaining
rep	repeat
RH	right hand

RS	right side
sl	slip a stitch
SM	slip marker from left to right needle
SS	stocking stitch
ssK	slip 2 stitches knitwise one at a time, pass the 2 slipped stitches back to the left-hand needle, knit both together through the back of the loop.
st(s)	stitch(es)
tbl	through the back of the loop
tog	together
w&t	wrap and turn (see techniques, page 12)
WS	wrong side
yo	yarn over needle

Easy Knitted Scarves — Monica Russel

Twenty to Make — Knitted Bears — Val Pierce

Knitted Pirates, Princesses, Witches, Wizards & Fairies with outfits & accessories

Introduction to Making Cloth Dolls — Jan Horrox

KNITTING FOR THE ABSOLUTE BEGINNER — Alison Dupernex

Twenty to Make — Tiaras & Hairpins — Michelle Bungay

Knitted Fairies to cherish and charm — Fiona McDonald

Twenty to Make — Mini Christmas Knits — Sue Stratford

Twenty to Make — Crocheted Beanies — Frauke Kiedaisch

Twenty to Make — Knitted Beanies — Susie Johns

Dress up your Dolls — Lise Nymark

CROCHET FOR THE ABSOLUTE BEGINNER — Pauline Turner

Babes in the Wool — McDonald

Tasty Knits

Twenty to Make — Crocheted Flowers — Jan Ollis

Gothic Knits — Fiona McDonald

Little Bears to Knit & Crochet — Val Pierce

Knitted Fruit & Vegetables

Flowers to Knit and Crochet — Susie Johns & Jan Ollis

Baby Booties and Socks

FOLLOW US ON:

twitter
www.twitter.com/searchpress

To request a free catalogue, go to http://www.searchpress.com/catalogues